Mental Matrix

The Puzzle Of Illusion

By

Kevin jr. And Shamil Cole

Copyright © 2017

Introduction

In this book we will cover how at times most of us feel as if we need to be and give more of ourselves. Sometimes we are mentally blocked and set in our own ways, and potentially get off course of our true paths. Confusion can sometimes settle in and cause the very problem that we need to work through. As people we need to stay on the right path, enjoy learning new things, and attaining a destiny that we may not see right away. Material things can also alter this path, thinking that we need tangible items to maintain our lifestyles.

Chapter One: Positive Thinking

True peace can't attained by simply changing the psychology of the human mind. Life as we know is not without fears and doubts. Most of our common fears are based on selfishness, There is so much misunderstanding about the concept of fear. Doubts and fears sometimes are dependent on how we view the world and the material comfort afforded by the world. Instead of worrying about my fear, I will adopt the ability to take control of it. I am in control of my fear and I will overcome it. Fear is probably the single-most thing in our lives that hold us back from success. When you have fear dwindling beneath the surface of our mind, often it encourages doubt. Doubt usually encourages low-self esteem, confidence, which all holds a person back from successfully gaining in life. Being positive and telling yourself that you can do something like reaching that big dream you have for the future will change your attitude and make those dreams come true. Tell yourself that you can do it instead of thinking negative and let your self-think that the dream is too big you'll never make it that far, this is not true, you need more hard work from your self! You can't have a positive thinking and self talk if you're not happy with yourself. Think positive and tell yourself you are going to make these changes in order to be the kind of person in your dreams. Tell yourself that you're going to be a happy person today. Everyday you're going to learn to smile more, learn a new skill, and do something positive for yourself.

By positive thinking and self-talk, you can do anything you want to do with a little hard work and changes in your life style. One of the largest problems in the world is judging. Scores of people judge and rarely do they truly get to know the person they judge. For instance, a local girl, for years was condemned, called ungodly names, and about tenyears down the road people watched her behaviors and deeply apologized. While damaging was done, not one person over ten years had enough sense to stop judging. Judging causes the emotions to uproar, which leads to doubt, fear, and negative energy. If you want to live a longer, healthier, and happier life, stop judging others. Depression can be caused from not thinking positive. Your mind will tell you that you have no energy, to stay in bed all day or the house cleaning can wait until tomorrow. Don't let depression take over your life. Stay in touch with yourself and use your self-power in thinking positive. Our mental mind is where we store our intellectual, You benefit by enhancing your skill and improve your recognition. Take some time out of each day for you, Building your self-awareness will give you the tools and resources that will help you to develop your mental, physical, and spiritual states.

Build you self-actualization also. Mind puzzles decree assist you in recalling details by remembering words that you may have put aside. The understanding mind is the trick in knowing how to connect with your subconscious mind. Rather than allow your emotions to bring you hardship. Take control of your mental, spirit and physical states by directing the mind to positive thinking. When you feel overwhelmed, mediate, and allow your mind room to breathe. As mentioned above, there's talk about the mental puzzle. Sometimes we get confused as to what is needed of us. We spend alot of money on things we truly do not need, in order to feel a sense of happiness. Momentarily is what this material gain really means. Why should we shower ourselves with so many gifts to ourselves in order to alter what we really think and feel about ourselves? Are you materialistic, or a worldly person? If so, then you need to adjust your attitude. Materialistic people often struggle with financial burdens, since they often fail to set limits on their spending. Rather than striving to payoff bills, they may push back a bill and buy an item they wanted. You should see impulsive behaviors, because this is the problem causing you to go on a spending binge. Your desires are tainted also. You will need to reform your mental, physical, and spiritual being by considering programs that help you to manage your life. True happiness is within our inner selfs, we can't begin to look on the outside, because we will never be satified if we do.

One thing to remember is that self awareness is the best thing we can have in our possession. Many people avoid seriousness. When a conversation becomes serious a person might derail by laughing off the information, or else joking. While you may think this is a way to reduce stress, the fact is derailing only sets a person up for many falls to come. Sometimes you have to be serious and there is nothing wrong with it. While you may want to escape reality, the fact is one day you are going to wake and smell the hardcore facts of reality, and when it hits you in the face so hard, you will look back and wish you hadn't spent your life traveling on the wrong path. Did you know that what you put in your mind comes out in your habits and behaviors? Remember to change the things you can change, and let God change the things you cannot change. Although, you may feel that your on the right path, but to actually know when your not is when things begin to repeat themselves, we can all use some improvements. Your attitude plays a part in living healthier, longer, and happier. When you have a positive outlook or attitude it moves you to achieve your goals and plans to live longer, healthier, and happier.

Train your mind to relax and think positive. Train your mind to think only during wake hours. Try to focus on one task at a time, which will promote memory and relaxation. Do not worry, rather do something about it. The best rule of thumb when working to live healthier, longer, and happier is to realize who you are and accept it. Work on self-talk and positive thinking to improve your overall life. You have to be happy with yourself, and love yourself enough. We get caught up in thinking we have to have it all together, but were beautifully imperfect. Our own image should be acceptable to one self, is we really want to make great improvements we have to change the way we think about ourselves, and display a more authentic lifestyle. Infrequently when we strive for the power of optimism, we can reduce stress. Reducing stress will encourage complete advance of your mental, fleshly, and spiritual being. The bright outlooks are our powerful influences that can stress how we feel and what we can accomplish throughout our life. We all have a huge desire to be the best versions of ourselves, so therefore we can't allow the blockage of the mind to limit us to what's right and what's best for us to grow into the person we are created to be.

The mind is a powerful source that we want all learns to panel. Once we have gained that control, it is easier to obtain that level of optimism we all deserve. Let's face it, pessimistic views can add stress to our lives, hold us back from performing to our best abilities, and even cause relationships to fail. Our thinking habits act as from our customs, beliefs, and the things we observe around. This learning confirms our perspective on life. The mind is the single most confusing attitude of our lives. Sometimes this alone can cause us to travel on the wrong path for far too long. Training to reorganize your mind, listening and hearing to what affects your pilgrimage can assist you in positive self-image-transilience of mental, spiritual, and fleshly winning. Rather than clinging on influences, take control of you. It's a choice between creating happiness and just being plain old unhappy. Unhappiness is also caused by the negativity expressed towards other people. It is hard to get along with other people when the worst is assumed of them.

It is normal for a person to be defensive and realistic when dealing with people but when it gets out of hand, the negativity becomes hurtful and offensive. It pays to give people the benefit of the doubt. There are a handful of unhappy people that easily judge and mistreat others. This negativity, although expressed towards other people, can rub on oneself. It is very important to be aware of how negativity creeps into one's system because it becomes the root of all other terrible things that lead to unhappiness. With this being said, I think it's a perfect idea to be as happy as you can be! Goals in life change from time to time. As soon as one goal is achieved, a person usually moves on to the next one. But there is one common goal that binds humanity happiness. No one can ever dictate what makes a person happy but there are certain guidelines that one can follow to reach personal happiness. These general guidelines are meant to be flexible. They should be tweaked according to one's lifestyle, goals, and principles. You will find that a happy life is not a privilege. It is something that you work for. Happiness is a both a choice and a responsibility.

Recognizing the positive and recusant forces of our mind's power can benefit us by helping us to avoid unwanted feelings that can affect our life, so in other words you get to choose to be a better or bitter person. Understanding the way you think is of importance, but you also have to allow yourself to be open to the ideas of others, you may just learn something new, or maybe enhance the thinking of your own. To live an inspired life is to walk with an enhanced awareness of everyone and everything around you, to see divinity and delight in everyday people and events, and to infuse your environment with the same magical energy. Follow your deepest and highest dreams. Dare to jump out of the box of conventional thought. Clobber your bad habits. Defeat your deepest fears. Never say never to even the most impossible ideal. Persevere even in your darkest of hours. If you set out to plant inspired ideas in your life, you first have to get rid of bad habits the weeds of your mind. Not just remove them at the start, but continuously watch out for them.

Chapter Two: Exploring Self

Even the most brilliant of inspired thoughts will die in a forest of vices. Even one bad apple can ruin the basket. First you have to heal the hole in your soul. Treat yourself to a good movie and a good meal and the company of someone you love. Stop expecting perfection of yourself. Reforming the gray matter, and physical self involves exploring our subliminal and conscious mind and to join it so that the two labor in harmony. We must also call to mind that the mind is created up of emotions, second thought, visuals, and triggers. Sometimes it's very hard to control all the many thoughts that run through our minds. Have you ever just laid awake for most of the night just thinking? You want to get some sleep, but your mind is not ready to rest. You become restless the next day, not because you didn't get to bed on time, but you didn't sleep! We consciously having thoughts that maybe at some point during the day you may have forgot about, something like forgetting to pick something up from the grocery store, or what to have for dinner the next day. Or maybe your going through a difficult time, and are not sure what to do. In other words, your, mental, physical.

As you start to relax your mind, will open doors to learning you once thought you had forgotten. Thinking about all the storms, and how to overcome those storms can also keep you up very late at night. Once you find that motivation that you need to change, you will find yourself enjoying life and reaping the benefits of all the good choices that you have empowered yourself to make. There are also going to be times where you will mess up and make a bad choice, however, you will learn from your mistakes and you may even end up finding even more motivation for your actions. There is so much that you will learn from life and if you open yourself up to new possibilities you will never find yourself regretting. Regrets are wasteful too! Why should you allow a regret to hold you back when there is usually nothing you can do to make it right. When something bad happens, we have to find the positive in it and learn from the mistake and move on. The power of the mind is a tricky device and scarcely do we discover the source that aroused emotional responses such as antagonism, suspicion, or desire.

We have control over our own beliefs, traditions, behaviors, culture, and attitudes, hence for, living a productive generation we can take back our control of these emotions. To advancement power of the mind, we must act on thought and scene and come to an expression of acceptance to function daily. Sometimes we feature before we act, we often heed to problems in our path. Problems such as divorces, arguments, fights, spending binges, alcoholism, etc are generally weeded out when we deal with our emotions and subconscious, drawing near to a panoptic perceptive of our identities and forms. Being positive is a huge aspect of giving you empowerment. You need to be positive about life and your choices, as well as, the consequences. When you learn how to look on the brighter side, things will just seem to fall into place. You'll get a lot of self-esteem from this and you'll be able to truly empower yourself to do whatever it is that you feel you need to do. You see, you can change anything about yourself.

It takes alot of positive thoughts and actions. A day by day attitude is the best, because we know changes can't be completed overnight, but you can make a decision to make those changes as often as you need to. It is very important that everyone accepts change sometime in their life; this is the only way that you will ever be able to empower yourself become successful in life. It is very important that you accept life as it is and go with the flow because you will have a more satisfying life then if you were to ignore change. Empowerment and change is very important to your success in all aspects of your life. For you to use the empowerment to better your life, you need to make sure that you take away the negative. The negative side of things will bring you down, however, you will make sure that you keep the positive going and you'll be able to make things right for you. The use of empowerment is basically where you can take the negative in your life and make it more positive. You have no idea how much better you will feel about yourself when you stop focusing on the bad things in life and start focusing on the things that work for you in your life.

You will only be able to make something out of your life is you are able to overcome the obstacles and better your life with positive actions. Not only do you need to stay positive, but you also need to know what is right and what is wrong for you. You need to determine what actions you have to take when you see a roadblock. You need to have a plan for the negative things that are going to try to set you back. When you have a plan for the negative things you are able to make the positive out of it. The best thing that you need to do for yourself is to just make the best out of the worst and never let something bring you down or think that your dreams are worthless. Empowerment means that you need to learn how to think critically. You should learn how to feel what you think and use it towards getting the response that you are working for. You need to also be more assertive in life. Knowing what you want and going after it are two very different things. You should use your resources to make sure that you know what you want and how to make it happen for you and your happiness. I don't think happiness is too far away from any of us. It's all apart of the way we think.

Both good and bad decisions come from the mind. I perfer to speak of the good ones that come to mind, especially since we are all trying so hard to live better lives, and become better people. Sometimes your mind can talk you out of doing the things you need to do. It tells you your not good enough or you will never be more than you currently are. Thoughts don't always tell the truth, so it's up to you to make good thoughts work for you. Often at times, we second guess our good decisions because there not that easy to deal with. But truth is, all good decisions are hard. You want to know if you change the right things in your life, then good things will come to you. Over thinking is also apart of the mental matrix, you just want to sit in silence from time to time without too many thoughts passing through. There are ways to meditate in order to quite the mind. Some of us have a hard time doing things because of worry, stress, maybe even depression. The truth is God gave us natural instincts, we just have to believe in ourselves! When life affects your attitude, you must be willing to bend and ready to seek out an alternative path to being positive. Living an inflexible life is akin to standing in the middle of a hurricane.

No matter what you choose to hold onto, you will be blown away, and your plans will be changed for you. You must be willing to alter your methods and allow life to lead you to the places you are intended to go. The benefits of positive thinking are truly incredible. They can extend to every area of your life, and you will feel like a whole new person. The power of positive thinking is the power of transformation. When you think positively, the changes do not only occur within yourself. The rest of the world will respond to your new outlook as you radiate happiness and pleasant emotions. You will become not only a better person; you will also be a better person to be around. The power of positive thinking opens up a whole new realm of possibilities. You will discover the effects of maintaining positive thought seeping into all the areas of your life like water absorbed by a sponge. Nothing will remain unchanged as your newfound outlook and attitudes infect your mind, your surroundings and your family and friends with happiness and bring you success beyond your wildest dreams. You know that positive thinking improves your mental health. But did you know it can also improve your physical health?

The power of your thoughts are so strong, it can actually affect the way your body behaves. Why is there such great power in favorable habits to bring about change in our life? It's because when we decide to make good choices over bad choices it's so much more favorable and feels so much better to us. In fact, if you consider it, there are likely a great many things for which you may feel great gratitude the little plants in your windowsill, the knowledge about wellness that you've accumulated through studying, and even the fact that the sun will indeed arise tomorrow. The way we think, is not always the best, our actions are what shows characteristics. In fact, sometimes the way we think can lead to a more negative thinking process. For example, if you think you can't achieve something meaningful in life, you may just believe that, and the sad thing is that you have yet to try. The mind can talk you out of your dreams, because newly things are either uncomfortable or uncertain. Our minds can make us fear something that is unknown to us, familiar surrounds comfort us more so than things that appear to be unfamilar.

Chapter Three: Be Happy

Sometimes, when all our doubts, fears and insecurities wrap ourselves up, we always come up with the idea of "I wish I was somebody else." More often than not, we think and believe that someone or rather, most people are better than us when in reality, the fact is, most people are more scared than us. We all have our insecurities. Nobody is perfect. We always wish we had better things, better features, better body parts, etc. But life need not to be perfect for people to be happy about themselves. Self-improvement and loving yourself is not a matter of shouting to the whole world that you are perfect and you are the best. It's the virtue of acceptance and contentment. When we begin to improve ourselves, we then begin to feel contented and happy. Look at what you're looking at. Don't wrap yourself up with all the negativities of the world. In building self-esteem, we must learn how to make the best out of worst situations. The process of making positive thinking work for you begins with destruction, or at least a mild shift in your thought structure. In order to make room for new methods and ideas, you must first tear out all the old negativity patterns.

For some, this can be a gradual process: as you witness positive thinking work for you, one small step at a time, you will slowly clear out those good things only happen to other people thoughts, and be able to cultivate the seeds of change. Sometimes change is not always a bad thing, it can be a really good thing if we change our perceptive nature from negative to positive. Have you been keeping your journal? If you start to lose faith in the power of positive thinking, try looking back and reflecting on all that you have accomplished so far. Even if things are hard for you right now, you should have already proven to yourself that positive thinking works fairly well for being a bunch of crap. Don't be afraid to pile on a new load of fertilizer when your first crop doesn't make it all the way. Remember to always have a self talk, this can help out alot especially if you feel like giving up. You have to talk yourself out of that, because there's nothing that will make you productive if you feel the need to give up. Believing in yourself and your abilities is absolutely the most important thing you can do on your journey to positive thinking. It is critical to develop the self-confidence you need to carry you through to the realization of your goals.

Self-confidence is a bit different from self-esteem. Self-esteem refers to your feelings about yourself, your behaviors and your worth as a person. Self-confidence is your belief in your abilities and in the way you present yourself to the world. The actions of others are more likely to erode your self-confidence rather than your self-esteem. However, the two emotions have quite a bit in common. Both are measures of your inherent or developed belief in yourself- and both can be easily pushed off balance, resulting in either over-confident or defeatist behaviors that distance you from your ultimate objectives. Wouldn't it be loving if we all thought positively everyday? There surely would be more love for each other, and we would all support each other in ways that we need to. Everything we could possibly do starts with one single thought, and in my opinion it should be the very best thoughts you can ever think of. Did you also know that you can change your moods by the way you think? If you believe your in a bad mood, you will behave that way. If you believe your in a good mood, your actions will show that as well. We can always change our moods just by knowing that we deserve to be in a great mood, no matter what's going on in life.

In order to determine the best attitude for any given situation, you should take some time to decide the kind of person you want to be, and the image you want to convey. You may be interested in being the life of the party, the quintessential sympathetic ear, or the strong and silent type with the ability to take the lead at any moment. Once you are aware of your true self, you can begin to adjust your attitude to match. The way you treat other people is a reflection of your own attitude. You cannot expect to sustain a positive attitude by acting negatively toward others. Even if your positive mood is not returned, you must strive to retain a sense of dignity and enthusiasm. Eventually, those who begrudge your happiness will either give in and join you, or give up and go away and in either case, you will be rid of the negative influence without stooping to negativity yourself. Your mind becomes fresh. When you have a fresh mind, you can move to unlock your mind power to attract success, money and friends. You want to choose good friends when your success comes your way. Rather than accepting any person that says they're your friend, find friends that give you something, rather than take from you.

Emotional battles will hinder you from succeeding, especially if you allow them. Instead of letting the negative feelings tear your success away, fight back. Emotional responses are not always bad, so recognize the good emotions when they come along. Again, when you commence to express doubt, sit down and ponder about what is causing your doubt, or fear to emerge. By thinking positive and taking control of your mind, you can become the person you want to be by unlocking the person hidden in the back of your mind. Take time now to explore your subliminal to relieve stress and unlock your mind power. Readjusting is the start to unlock your mind power. Everyone needs goals to stay active to keep our brain working and learning. Our brain needs to be active or it will forget what it has already learning than our memory will slowly go to sleep. Staying active with goals will exercise the brain to make it keep learn new skills and to function on a daily basis. It take a lot of hard work to change old habits believe me but be positive and tell yourself that you can and will do it. Tell yourself that the old habits are out the door and bring in the new positive habits.

Write them down so make them seem more real by reading and reading them repeatedly. The more writing and reading you do you'll make your brain believe that you can do this and than it will pitch in to help. Old habits can be devastating, leading to nothing but a damaging state of mind, restricting you from positive change. I understand that it takes alot if time and practice to be happy on a daily bases, because somethings make us as human feel disappointed. It's not impossible to want happiness, it's a mind change that needs to take place. It's a really good habit to speak those great things over yourself soon as you awake in the morning, just to ensure that a good day is what you desire to have. Eventually a pattern of good habits and good self talk will become a regular thing to do. We have to remove negative talk daily, it sometimes tries to get in the way of having a good day and being in a positive mood, but as I mentioned it's not impossible to attain, as the old habits, disappear. Moreover, the positive habits start taking over you will enjoy being alive again and happy to go to work. Taking care of yourself and changing old negative thoughts to good positive ones will bring out the real you. Learning how to free yourself from bad habits starts with the realization that we cause our own feelings. I am the major cause of my own problems. The moment I grasp that simple fact, I'm ready to step into the process of self-change that will lead to freedom from the habits that keep me from living a more satisfying life.

And when I'm free from my bad habits, the people around me will be free from the person I used to be. All people can bring about superficial changes in themselves. But freeing yourself from a selfdestructive habit like smoking or overeating requires a deep, long-lasting change. A bad habit is like an iceberg. You can't beat the habit if you approach it as if it were only as large as what you can see on the surface. The key to freeing yourself from bad habits is to change your lifestyle. A total lifestyle change isn't something that happens overnight. It happens one day at a time, as soon as you begin to focus on the solution instead of the problem. The process of total lifestyle change starts when you begin to think more about the present than the past. Our conscious notice the negative things and stores them later to use. The conscious mind programs the subconscious to tell us what to do. Your conscious mind pick up these things to use and you don't even realize it because it used what it hears and can see. If the entire conscious mind is hearing negative things all the time that is all it is going to know. The key to freeing yourself from bad habits is to change your lifestyle.

A total lifestyle change isn't something that happens overnight. It happens one day at a time, as soon as you begin to focus on the solution instead of the problem. The process of total lifestyle change starts when you begin to think more about the present than the past. I know what your thinking, this is hard to do right? It's the process in getting started that makes this step seem so hard. Lifestyle changes happen everyday, because we all grow daily. If were afraid to change, then the first step to this it to aware yourself of the reasons why you have this fear in the first place. What happens when fear meets a sense of depression? Defeating depression is difficult, maybe the most difficult thing you'll ever do. Opposing depression isn't a stroll in the park; it's a dogfight. But if you choose to join the fight, you can win the struggle. Your emotions are an expression of your thoughts. When you alter your ideas, your emotions automatically alter. You don't have to fight the negative and bent emotions repeating in your brain. Rather, you need to learn how to alter the way you think, and emotions will by nature take care of themselves. Like dark follows daylight, when your views are healthy and favorable, your emotions become healthy and favorable as well. If you have come to the realization that you're stuck in a self-defeating lifestyle, you have already taken the first step in the cycle of self-change. You have started to become aware of the need to change in some area of your life.

Chapter Four: Subconscious Thinking

Listen to yourself if your thinking negative your subconscious will help you to continue. The subconscious lives for whatever it has been told by the negative or positive thoughts. We can learn with practice to change the subconscious to think positive with a little effort on our part. Your willingness to acknowledge the areas that need change in life, is another big to becoming a better person! Mix this with self discipline you can change many things in your life, whatever it is that can help you succeed and feel good about yourself. Our mind picks up things especially the negative thoughts from other people. Subconsciously we hear them as feedback when we are doing things making us think negative. Learn to overcome the negative and become positive with self-talk. Also, During depression the individual seems to get pessimistic. The therapy helps to alter the pessimistic thoughts as well as the unrealistic expectations. Occasionally critical self evaluation may likewise cause depression. I understand that sometimes life can seem hard, and overwhelming. You get the sense of feeling like nothing going right, and all the odds are against you, and it takes alot of inner searching and healing to make this feeling go away. We can also be so tough on ourselves without understanding how patient we need to be within. Unlock your mind power with self-talk to by telling yourself that you will think positive. Remember that this needs to take place daily in order to have better results and solutions to those problems life can bring.

Trust those powers exist. The opening move to utilizing brain power is to trust it lives. Trust is the key. If you don't trust in the power of the brain, it is not going to work out for you. How may you expect something to work out if you don't trust it can? Your auto won't start if you don't put the key in the ignition system and turn it on. Trust is the key that switches on your awesome brain power. You need to be objective. This means that you need to think about the things that you want in life and know how to get them. When you are willing to make a motion and get what you want, you will find that you will feel better inside and out. Your body will have the power to go after what your mind wants and this is a form of physical empowerment. Sounds exciting right? Yes, it is! Physical empowering tools are all ready there for you, utilizing this tool properly is very important.   What if you've passed your whole life up to this level with all the huge decisions being arrived at a much smaller level of consciousness than you're capable of? What if you've been arriving at the huge conclusions out of fright because you didn't recognize how to exercise your true bravery? What experiences are perpetually refused you because your awareness operates at too modest a level? If you had no dread, would you yet live your life as you do today? If not, what would you alter? Although, it can be very hard to stay in a postive mindset, especially when things can seem so negative, and sometimes it's hard to understand that both negative and positives things accur, just remember that we all have a choice, and those choices should be extremely positive.

The creative power inside us makes us into the mental image of that to which we provide our attention. The thankful mind is perpetually fixed upon the most beneficial; consequently it will get the most beneficial. Do you understand what I'm saying? If we're grateful and appreciative about everything, we're centering on what we require. It's a way of making a point that we're placing the greatest possible positive energy on our wants, and keeping energy from the uncertainties and fears that we don't wish for. Another good thing to remember, is to stop living in the past. Many live in the past tense. We dream about what may have been. We all live in the past tense occasionally. Particularly when we get with old acquaintances. But, when your thoughts are largely in the past that may really make a damaging impact on your life. When you keep conjuring up the past and re-experiencing the past repeatedly, it makes a damaging impact on relationships. Remember worrying about the time to come or regretting the past isn't going to alter what has or is going to happen. Don't let yourself worry. Worrying consumes all your energy and keeps, you stressed out. Stand back from damaging conversations with yourself. Be cognizant of your thoughts. Stop projecting what is going to happen as it never happens the way you believe it will anyway. Don't consider tomorrow nothing ever happens the way you might think it will.

Except the fact that you'll have great and bad moments even terrible moments have a purpose. Escaping the moment is tantalizing when it feels objectionable. Regardless if the moment you're having right now is pleasant or objectionable it's still yours. Deciding not to live it, is casting aside a part of your universe your life. Have faith you'll then have the strength to live all of them, not only the pleasurable ones. Living in the present moment, you're free from your past and free from your concerns of the future. To be really present; it involves you having absolute trust in yourself; trust that nothing that happened in the past will mess with your future. Likewise, trust yourself with the future after all you came through this far in life. Trust that time will take care of all cares, fears and everyday life. Arrive at a conscious decision to forgive somebody. Even if they never apologize for what occurred, settle within yourself that it's okay to proceed without this apology. Apologies shouldn't be about permission to us to forgive somebody. Apologies should be provided as an effort of honest remorse and acknowledgement that taking personal responsibility for the situation is crucial. Even without that apology, reconcile your mind to forgive, forget, and finally let go. Sometimes, we as human being confuse our wants with our needs, letting go of the past is hard because we want things to remain the same, but in reality it's our needs that tend to suffer. A want is comforting, a need is uncomfortable, leading us to hold tight to a painful past.

The past can be painful, and has to be something we learn to let go of, in order to be opened to the new, which is usually what we need anyway. Why must we be so stubborn, and fearful of change? Learning to separate the wants from the needs will be the best way to understand. Take a sheet of paper and pencil and put down a list of your positive qualities and what you admire about yourself. Write in flow of consciousness style. Try not to hesitate. Author whatever you think you shine at. For the bulk of our waking lives we get so tripped up in the negative aspects of ourselves. Too many people fear change, and change is inevitable. So instead of fighting it, reach out and grab it, holding it close because it's truly something to learn from. Keep on in control of your continuance; don't let your life take ever and control you. By understanding yourself and mind, you learn how to find yourself, see what has gone wrong, and fix it. You want to avoid setting traps for your memory and intelligence, since the emotions to enjoy run-down races if you allow it. What I mean is you want to halt telling yourself I cannot do it. Life is too hard. Life is having a sigh of relief if you learn to think productive. Instead of supporting your emotions, allowing them to bring you privation. Take control of your character, spirit, and physical by conducting the mind to explore the positive winnings of your history. Start with meditation and natural breathing practices to succeed. Breathing routines can collaboration you with assuagement too!

There is someone very close to you, who has been either inspiring you or depressing you throughout your days. It's your Subconscious. Your intuitive mind. You are often so busy with your conscious self that you forget that the mover and shaker of all your thoughts and deeds lies deep within you. Your subconscious mind has been receiving inputs from your conscious mind since the day you were born. Good and bad experiences, all the books you read, the songs you heard, the praise and damnation you have received, they all sink slowly through the film of your consciousness into your inner core. It is the good stuff that rises to spur you on to great achievements, but if negative messages have been accumulated for too long, they too will reach out and drag you down. If the Subconscious is empty or hurt, it cannot give you great results. So feed it with good literature, music and loving realtionships. It will grow healthy and powerful within you. Our lives are assembled of the building blocks of change. Change produces the individual we must grow to be. Remember we mentioned the wants verses the needs? This is the perfect example because all too often were more inclined to be satified by those wants, and that will not get us out of the mental matrix.

Frequently, in any situation, we must take the calm time to be with ourselves to note this change. How is it going to affect me? Better yet, how am I going to let it effect me? What am I going to do to come through this? Let the answers to come to you in your calm time. Change displays itself in a lot of forms. The move to another career, by choice or not, the loss of a loved one, the loss of a relationship, the move to a new house or merely the change in the weather and how we experience it. Accept everything one day at a time. Occasionally situations may become consuming when viewing the big picture. Again, take your calm time to note the moment. Allow yourself to take all the time, take the space that you require to grasp the alteration. Love Yourself. You're the true source to your own felicity. You have to live inside yourself. You have to be at serenity within yourself. Only you are able to do that. Only you are able to make that happen. We each have our own style of being with ourselves, but there's only one way to be at rest with your soul. That's to love yourself, always. To love yourself, is to love others, and help others. It's our job as human being to uplifts those around us. But, this is not something you can do with a negative mindset.

Apart from that if you start feeling worthless you will start neglecting yourself as a person and will stop caring about how you look and that will even start affecting your health. Stress will be the order of the day in your life if you are always feeling negative and that may cause migraine headaches. If your negative attitude starts rubbing off on other people then you have great reason to worry because if you friends or colleagues all feel the same way that you do then you all will not be able to overcome the feelings. Being surrounded by negative people is very dangerous because they will not try and make you see the best in you. Instead of bringing your spirits up when you are down they will further agree with you that you are incapable of being better and that you cannot do anything positive. When we are in a negative state we do not attract those elements that would make our lives advance; rather we attract the circumstances that support us in thinking something is wrong, and we get stuck. Simply put, when we stay thinking negative, we attract negative emotions and events. Thus when one is in a negative state everything seems to go wrong. This kind of situation will not help you in anyway and you cannot be a better person among negative people.

Chapter Five: What's Familiar

When we relinquish the familiar, we have the mightiness to embrace the fresh. Be pliant. You have a rigid, mind set about work, relationships, youngsters or life-style. Learn a lesson from the willow and its power to bend in the great wind. Where as, when we're rigid like the old oak, we may easily break up under the stress of change. Learn to loosen up and follow the path stretching out before you. It's there to guide you through life, human being think they have the answers to everything, therefore making it harder to learn new things, you should always remain a student of life. Each and everyday is a new one, and there's plenty of things we have yet to learn. By opening the mind you will find that maybe you really didn't have your life all figured out, and that it's perfectly okay to listen to others that have the experience and knowledge of which is lacked. So take just a few minutes today, and do a kindness for another person. It can be something small or the start of something big. Ask them to pay it forward. Put a smile on someone's face. Smile and be friendly. better. They could then do the same for other people.

Help somebody on the edge. If somebody is suicidal, urge them to get help. If they do not, call a suicide hotline or physician yourself to get advice. Just be there. When someone you know is in need, sometimes it's just good to be there. Sit with them. Talk. Help out if you can. Be patient. Sometimes people can have difficulty understanding things, or learning to do something right. Learn to be patient with them. A hug, a kind word, spending time, showing little kindnesses, being friendly, it all matters more than you know. Some of us just go through life mad at the damn world. Why hold onto anger, bitterness, rudeness and just plain out mean as hell? Our thinking is the only thing that can change our lives, our perpective in the way we see things really need some adjustment. None of us want to spend the rest our of lives hating someone and being selfish to the point where it's affecting our core being. This will leave you in the mental matrix, because your too stubborn to change old habits and thinking patterns. Someone else could teach you a thing or two if only you would listen . No you are not crazy or going crazy, you just need to free your mind, and understand that we all have problems, and things we would like to change in our personal lives.

Among the primary ways we can help other people to accomplish new inner growth is by outgrowing ourselves to help others go higher. To help us understand the wisdom in this new idea we must first think about additional equally important ideas. A good portion of the way we "see" ourselves is actually a provision of our relationships with acquaintances and loved one. For example, much of the way we evaluate the value of ourselves is secretly affiliated to those values we attribute to other people close to us. Understanding these truths mandates that we back off from being secretly on everyone's back, that we give them the inner room they need to grow and discover themselves. The difficulty here is that in order to give others this space they need, we must first make room within ourselves. To state this same idea differently, we must remove ourselves from our habitual inner places of judgments, opinions, and knowing better than anyone else. We have always called this place that must be left behind our "self." It's crucial in life to help others in life. In essence, not only does it make us feel good, it makes the other party feel good. It gives you a sense of fulfillment, and also creates a better feeling for the individual you're helping.

You have to be truly "satisfied" if you're going to switch on your brain and, therefore, powered up to learn. All the same, there are a few aspects of the way in which the brain works that may deter you from reflecting on your errors. So, for instance, the negative consequence of stress on the brain means that it may be really hard to work in places where reflection and admission of failure are not imaginable. Concerns build up and performance levels go down. As your brain is a pattern-making mechanism, it's often done its reflection without your being consciously cognizant of it. So, you might be able to wake up the morning after something has happened with a clearer feel of its meaning. Effective reflection calls for you to be open and exploratory. It's likewise crucial not to be defensive and not to take things personally. In the context of learning to learn, it's your capacity to reflect on how you approached learning something that you'll find particularly useful. If you're going to develop fresh techniques, you have to review the way you do things and check how they work for you, understanding that they way things work for you, do not mean it will work for someone else, it's all apart of doing the best for you, and still helping others in return.

Understandably, we all have been through a ton of different things in life, some good and bad. Our life experiences are what makes us who we are. Something tragic can happen an change our entire lives, and we may never fully recover from that emotion. Our mind tries to move us past that pain and sometimes we tell our minds the total opposite of what it's telling us. For example, if you are tired of crying about something that happened years ago, you may command your mind to let it go. We can choose to be in whatever mood we want to be in, but the real question is "Do we really want to be in a horrible mood"? What if we have great things happening but have hungon to the past for so long that we actually forget the good that surrounds us? Be truthful with yourself and other people. It is time to get truthful. Truly ... life is too short. Your life is yours, and yours to live only. Your journey is personal to you, and only you. Focus extremely hard on the good things, but at the same time, they'll try to get you to return back to your old habits. Do not! Trust that you've made the most healthy and most beneficial decisions conceivable, and stand firmly planted. In the final analysis you will start to feel freedom and a sense of regard for yourself. Time , what a treasured asset. To a few individuals, it's the most valuable commodity of all. And all the same we never seem to have enough of it. Our days are occupied with work, family responsibilities, errands, and home chores. A couple of easy changes may free up minutes a day, hours a week. Make the selection and change your life!

Start Visualizing what it is in life you really want to do. Mental images are often created through brainstorming or meditating. When we brainstorm or meditate while conjuring up mental images, it inspires the mind. We develop plans, and design from this action. Moreover, we can take initiative action by picturing in our mind what we must do. Relaxation eases your mind, thus it helps you to take up again creating mental pictures in your mind and you can start in on thinking optimistically. We all must give the mind room to breath so we can think positive in order to profit from visualizations and affirmatives. Many people miss the benefits of meeting the inner self. The inner self is the entire being within each of us that sets us free from burden, distress, illness and other harms. We have the inner strength, which is the inner self that allows us to draw from its source to find ways to develop the entire human being. Yet, we have many things to consider. We have to discover our self-identity throughout the process of development. Because so many people fail to recognize the degree of self-development that has taking place throughout their life, it is imperative to spread out your self-awareness and conscious mind. By building these traits and skills, one can start to recognize the body and mind's activities, which makes it easier to spot details that develop through visualizations in the mind. These visual aids are your assistant agents that will work with you to create affirmatives that guide you to positive thinking.

Chapter Six: Mental Info

The mind will use the information in some order to resolve problems. On the other side, many people struggle for a long time to find answers to solve their problems, because they fail to assist the mind with question and evaluating the information learned. We must develop skills that assist the mind with finding answers to problems. Some of the best ways to build these skills is through continuous learning, willingness, observation and questioning the self consistently throughout our life. Visualization and affirmation is also essentially needed in order to develop skills that assist the mind with problem solutions that lead to discovery. Understand other people. If you know how to talk, you ought to also learn how to listen. Envision it. Motivation without imagination is like a boat on the ground. Want it more than anything. Dreaming means trusting. And to trust is something that's rooted in motivation and confidence. We achieve a point in our life when we're ready for change and a whole bunch of data that will help us unlock our confidence.

And just when you're enjoying the whole procedure of unlocking your confidence, you'll recognize that you're beginning to take the correct steps for self betterment. We can learn how the mind works to take effective action in reshaping the mind. At what time one can identify the actions of his or her mind by using original systems that help one to conceive that the mind is a repetitiously revolving mechanism. Throughout our lifetime, we all go through life's vicissitudes that causes us pain. Many people fail to resolve the issues by finding cause of the pain. We can always use affirmations and visualizations to discover problems and find ways to resolve these problems. Our mind and body takes us through a life long series of processes in which it works to repair any damage that we lived. One can invigorate the mind and body to live a better life. When you live genuinely, you might find that you develop an interrelated sense of being. When you're true to whom you are, living your passion and giving of your talents to the world around you, you repay in service what you came to share with other people your spirit your essence. Sharing your gift with those close to you is so rewarding.

Confidence is indeed one type of work that's worth it. It shouldn't always be inside the confines of an office building, or in your room. The difference lies inside ourselves and how much we wish to change for the better. Treat yourself as you'd treat other people. Do not be so hard on yourself. Chances are you wouldn't tell others that they're fat, ugly, lazy, dense, un-needed, and so forth. So don't verbally beat yourself up. You need to regard yourself as much as you respect other people. If you've a habit of putting yourself down now is the time to alter it. Stop putting yourself down, and stop trying to please everyone. You need to be happy too, and you deserve to be! You might look at people who have absolutely everything and you strive to be like them. These things may be wealth, possessions, status, or even the position you hold at work. These things don't create happiness. Happiness is a choice.Be more good-hearted to yourself by shedding damaging relationships. Circle yourself with the individuals that love, appreciate, and support you. Weed out the individuals that bring you down. Life is too short for toxic relationships.

There, in all likelihood, aren't very many of us out there who truly and sincerely give back to ourselves nearly enough. How often do you schedule time just for you or take care of your health? In all likelihood not that much. We take care of everyone else, but rarely commit any time to doing anything nice for ourselves. If you've been stripping yourself of "you" time and taking care of your health, you should alter that, beginning right now. You may think you can't squeeze in any more extra time for anything, not to mention time to do something just for you. But you're incorrect. You'll be able to find time if you would like to. Now, what should you do? Take care of your health. Everyone seeks happiness in their own way. What makes you happy is a natural high that you deserve to seek. There is nothing wrong with the things that you find joy in. You may be told you are crazy but that is because of the subjectivity. Many people find themselves in situations where they have fallen into a situation where they are not doing as they wish they were. They go to work because they have to not enjoying a single day of it. If you started over again would you take advantage of the new beginning or would you go back to where you are? What would you do?

Many people have dreams they wish to pursue but they never attempt to move forward with the dreams because they cannot afford to get started. Think of what you would love to do if you had the money to do it. This can be anything. Name all of the things that have caused you to not follow your big dreams. These things could be people who do not support you, money, fears, and other things. There are many different types of barriers which can be overcome. You might not see opportunity or success with your dreams or you may fear that people would make fun of you. You might not even be skilled and lack talent. These could be barriers causing you not to move forward.Everyone is good at something. If you don't have a hobby like making candles, beaded jewelry, or working on cars on the weekends it doesn't mean you don't have a skill. This just means that you haven't quite figured out what your skill is yet. You need to know what it is that interests you the most. The majority of people are very good at what they do when they enjoy it. Curiosity helps create an active mind. When someone is curious they always ask questions and seek for the answers. The causes their mind to be active most of the time. When you are curious and working the mind you are making it stronger. Your brain is like a big muscle and by working it you are making it much stronger. Curiosity also allows you to see how things can be at different angles. When you are set in one way things are limited because your mind is not willing to accept a different solution. It is much like your life. If you don't see your life becoming any more successful than it already is then you won't be.

If you can open your eyes to new ideas about how things can be then you are more willing to try them. The great thing about curiosity is that when ideas do come to your mind they will be recognized also and not ignored. When you are not curious you miss out on the important ideas because you haven't prepared your mind to be open to them. This also means you must be open to suggestion. Many people offer input that you might not want to hear. This input could have been the one thing that was what you needed to do in your life. Be open to suggestion by allowing yourself to ask more questions and seek different answers. The biggest barrier to someone not fulfilling their passion and dreams is another person. It is common for someone to add input that is hard to listen to because you feel like you are being made fun of. A person may ridicule the idea, think it is silly, and much more. The last thing you need to listen to is an outside opinion if it is negative. If you have a passion you need to surround yourself with supportive people. Someone who is not supportive is not who you want around because they will only bring you down. That is, if you let them. Now we can start to brainstorm to find potential solutions that help us solve the problems. Brainstorming can help you come up with brilliant ideas to solve the problem. Brainstorming allows you to come up with diverse solutions that fit or are relevant to the problem. You can devise the problems by making suggestions and thinking through each problem effectively and with a clear mind.

We all go through changes in our lifetime. Some of the changes are good and many are bad, yet we must continue to thrive toward a positive future. It takes us to use visualization and affirmation to keep the mind encouraged and looking for something brighter. We must also learn to accept change. Change is what helps us to grow stronger and happier. When we see change as a positive instead of a threat to the emotions, it often helps us to visualize grander days. Many people create mental images in their mind however. It is good that they create mental images, but they also should use affirmation to thrive toward developing a positive mind. At some time in our life, we all confront situations that push us to make good decisions. Often we have to use our persuasive voice to convince others that we can do something. It could be through writing, verbal communication, or other method that we have to persuade someone of our ability. Effective arguments usually start with ideas that we create in the mind. We often have a basis for these ideas. For this reason, we need to practice visualization in order to offer supports to our claims. Fear is another one of the biggest reasons people do not move forward.

By the power of curiosity you will be more open to suggestions and know that there can be a better outcome than what your mind has limited you to believe. You might even have a fear of success. That might sound funny but many people are afraid to succeed. They have problems saving money and as soon as they start saving up enough to start their dream they spend the money on something they don't even need. Later they are kicking themselves and begin the saving process all over again. You should never be afraid to succeed. This fear is natural and many people have a self esteem low enough they don't believe they are good enough to be successful. You can be as successful as you really believe you can be. Don't let your fears of what could be getting in the way. Our behaviors often hinder us from lucratively achieving our goals. That is, perhaps you are a couch potato. If so then you are not working in the direction of spiritual, mental, or physical development. When we deal with problems now, as an alternative of putting them off, and learn to control the interferences can help us to learn to manage our life effectively.

Chapter Seven: Mind And Body

When we do not encourage our mind and body to take action, it over and over again leads to big headaches. Often we may find ourselves struggling to focus on one task. When we review our progress, sometimes we see the things we had forgotten. From the foundry, and capital, we must continue to focus on our duties to prevent falling into a pattern that will lead us nowhere. When you start to battle common problems in mental, spiritual and self-development, you must have priorities in place. Put priorities in order by organizing your life, focusing on time management and so on. You want to create workable plans, and push your priorities to the front, so that you can stroll along the same patterns of the human mind through. When you put procrastination behind you, you tend to focus on what matters the most. When you struggle with bills, instead of delaying take action now to resolve your debts. When you are trying to control your weight, try to turn up nutritive facts, and construct a workable plan that will fit your lifestyle, and commence today to put the ball in motion. The most deeply possible way to build your mind and body is common approaches, such as exercise.

When you give your mind and body what it needs, you will find enjoyable rewards. The closer you get to achieve your true passion the more ambition you will have to live out the dream and make it happen. If you need to brush up on your skills first then take a few classes. These classes will be a part of your milestones and steps to get to where you want to get to. As you complete each one then you will have completed a milestone and closer. Your passion needs to make you whole. You need to focus on not just one thing but every aspect of your passion. Enjoy the experience in its entirety. Enjoy the process of ordering the parts and having them delayed for two weeks. This could mean a wonderful vacation for you while you are waiting rather than a sign you weren't supposed to get started on your passion. Don't look at negative things happening as a sign. Be whole with everything you do. Don't try to be fake or impress someone with someone you are not. Your attitude could make you or break you. You need to maintain a complete positive attitude. Be positive at all times. Don't let the little things get you down or upset you. You are living your passion and every obstacle now is a learning experience.

Now you need to have a positive outlook on everything you do with your business and your passion. When you have a good attitude it will help you become more successful with your business and your passion. You need to have a positive outlook and believe. When your attitude is positive and your outlook is positive things will begin to work in your favor more often than they ever have before. It is really about the way you look at things and not how bad they really are. You make things and a situation bad. Your attitude is what will make it positive. The best way to build momentum when you are working toward your passion is to act on the ideas you have. Act right away and don't sit around for something to happen or come to you. The same goes for a problem you need to fix. You need to act on it. The more responsive you are then you begin to build a momentum that is hard to break. Your laziness will go away and you will do well with being more productive. So many folks hammer away, trying to focus on insignificant aspects of their life. Often it robs them of time they could spend on developing their skills through visualization and affirmation.

Start today to reprogram the mind by considering your goals on how you plan to succeed in the development process through visualization and affirmation. Look at your inner feelings to decide how you feel about yourself and how you can change them for the better. Ask yourself; are you happy with your looks, career and performance? Write your goals and changes on paper and keep them close at all times. Try to recite each day so that you benefit from your goals and plans. In time, your positive changes will override the negative thoughts to help you be successful for reaching your goals. It makes no sense to let our inner strengths go to waste. Sorry to say, but many people tend to let this happen. Many people sit on the settee watching soaps, drinking cocktails, eating popcorn and wasting priceless time. They could be out in the authentic world getting their groove on through exercise, goal affirmation, diet, self-development and visualization. In spite of everything, it takes you to make it happen. You want to tap into those inner strengths and find your weaknesses so that you can develop skills that help you to grow strong and healthy. Life is too short to keep putting off self-development.

When you live out your true passion in life you will also need to accomplish a few more things. You must give your life to something, be free from pain, not focus on results, and not worry about survival issues. When you give your life to something you immediately dedicate yourself to the passion. This means you will need to give as much time and energy possible to your passion. The rest will follow naturally as you are dedicated and entirely given to your passion. The pain and pleasure principle does not count when it comes to working toward a passion. Your passion may give you pleasure as it makes you happy and you love to do it. However, reaching your goals may be painful and frustrating. You may cry at times and want to throw in the towel. Success is never easy but you would very much rather work toward a passion than you would go to a job you hate every single day. This passion is yours and you own it. Feel the pain and make it satisfying in every way. The pain will satisfy your soul which is much better in the long run because you will not have any regrets later on. Never concentrate on results. The universe is going to take care of the results. Things might be slow at first and if all you are looking at is the results then you may never get there. Focus on what you need to do and you will find the your way.

Never worry about survival when you are working toward a passion. This is the most important key to be successful with a passion. When you worry or have fear you will create problems for yourself. You need to have courage in your heart and your mind that you will be fine and you really will. As human beings, we all need to have goals in life to keep us happy in everything we do. When we do not have dreams or goals, it causes us to miss our purpose. When we lose sight of our purpose, it becomes harder to take action when opportunity comes our way. Writing is a structure of mental implement. By writing, a journal or your life story it will alleviate stress and you will be using your mental state of mind as well. Writing can help with visualizing your future. When you write it helps you to explore the mind to find new ideas. You can make new discoveries by learning from your past-experiences. Use your knowledge and experience so you can get feedback to encourage you to live an affirmative lifestyle. You can reduce stress by writing down your goals. Learn how to change your life to be a successful person. Writing gives you many benefits.

Inside the mind lies, a power resource that provides us the tools we need to develop new skills through affirmation and visualization. We must find our way in life, so dip into your mind and take a stroll down subliminal lane where you will find answers to all your questions. These answers are there to help you solve your problems while developing your skills. Our perceptions either help us to gain or lose control. It locks up, hiding in our subconscious mind and reflects on our lives. Visualizations or mental images are an illustration of this hidden mind taking action. If you have a true passion and you have obstacles stopping you from achieving living the dream then you must get past them and you can. Anyone can be successful with a passion. They can turn it into their own personal business easily if they want to. If you want to work towards making things in your life happen for you, it is possible and you can do it. Don't get discouraged because the task seems daunting, it's more than doable when you realize you're potential. You just need to be able to set aside some time each day to reflect on your life and yourself and to use those ideas and feelings to motivate you!

We are all able to make constructive changes, even if we feel like we're hopeless. If you have enough will power, the realization you want to change, and a positive outlook... the rest will follow suit shortly. You never have to go it alone, however, there are many beautiful and helpful guides and tricks to help you along the way, and all you have to do is seek them out. The main reason why people cannot accept change is that they fail to understand the nature of change. Many people still keep strong the beliefs of their ancestors. Change is disruptive, anarchistic and wrong. However, this is simply not the case; change is merely a logical progression of things. Change is the channeling of positive energy to bring about positive changes. If you take all of your positive and hopeful thoughts about owning a new washer and dryer and put them to use to motivate you into getting a promotion or a bonus at work, you have achieved change. What most people don't know is that the thoughts that occur in your mind are soon manifested in your habits and behaviors. If you are surrounded by violent and criminal behavior or crude and repulsive acts, you will begin to exude these tendencies and commit these acts.

Chapter Eight: Problem Solving

Relying on other people and even computer programs may seem like a quick and effective way to unload your problems but in reality, it's doing you more harm than good. By doing this, you are constantly avoiding the responsibilities and problems that you face in your life. If you are face-to-face with a problem you can't outsource, a problem that a computer can't fix, will you be prepared? Shirking all of your problems and responsibilities onto other people inhibits your ability to grow and learn as a person. As a result, you will be most likely stuck in a dead-end job that you hate, surrounded by people who you despise. Are you happy with who you are and what you do? If not, ask yourself why not. If you aren't happy with yourself, chances are this has a very negative impact on your life. There are many things you can do to improve your self-esteem and the way you see yourself. Take five minutes to write down on paper all of the things about yourself that you feel are unique or that you feel proud of. Now do the same with all of the things you feel are negative about you or bringing you down. Now take the list of negative things and burn it.

You should then proceed to hang the list of positive things somewhere in your house where you will see it every day. This will remind you of what a good person you can be and how much you are important. Relaxation doesn't necessarily mean having no problems; this is why people are unable to relax. People believe that in order to relax, their life has to be rid of anything that is problematic or stressful. While this would be ideal, it's simply not possible. This why people never get the results they want by unloading their problems on others and manifesting their stress into terrible habits. What you need to do is to take time to yourself each day. It doesn't have to be much, maybe only an hour. Use this time to do something that is cathartic, something that takes your frustrations and problems and channels them into something positive and relaxing. Take up jogging or boxing, start writing a novel; maybe even start a little business for you. The point is that you should be doing something that is fun for you and that you love.

Once you start relaxing and not constantly worrying about the problems in your life, solutions to these problems will emerge. You will begin to think clearer and you mind will not be so crowded with negative thoughts. This will allow the emergence and free passage of positive thoughts and interesting ideas. You can now harness this power to bring about positive and constructive changes in your life. Through practice and planning, we have the power to train the subconscious psyche, reinforcing it to adapt to new changes. We have the ability to train the subliminal mind. Positive thinking is a powerful tool for self-reliance and constructive change. For many people, positive thinking is the key to unlocking long-term happiness and satisfaction. In order to experience constructive change in life, you must develop the self-reliance that comes as a result of positive thinking. Positive thinking is necessary to incorporate constructive changes in ones life. Fully to enjoy the benefits of self-reliance, positive thinking is necessary. Positive thinking is strongly linked to self-awareness. Through positive thoughts people are able to discover who they are at the core, and find their inner selves and hidden strengths.

Positive thinking will helps us make changes necessary for lifelong success and happiness, and guides us in the right direction toward having a positive outlook on life. Great deals of the attitudes we develop toward life develop subliminally, which means that we do not consciously decide to have the attitudes that we have. The way that we think and view the world affects our overall attitude. Negative thinking leads to a negative outlook. Positive thinking influences the development of positive emotions and reactions to feelings. This is how positive thinking can lead to constructive change. You are the only person who can change your own behavior. Once you make a decision to change, you will have an easier time sticking to your decision if you come up with a set of strategies designed to keep you from losing your willpower. Many times, the secrets to changing your behavior lie in your subconscious mind. By reflecting internally, you may be able to discover solutions to behavior change that are buried within your subconscious. You may also want to do some external research of willpower and behavior change. There are many books and Internet resources that provide this type of information.

However, simply becoming aware of barriers to change or the secrets of how to change isn't enough to bring about change. You have to make a decision and take action to bring about change on your won. Everyone has daily stress. There is nothing we can do but learn to thrive on him or her. There is some stress that we can eliminate to help lessen the heavy load when breaking bad habits. Use your self-talk and ask yourself why you feel the need to smoke or binge eats. Think about the consequences of your actions. This is what prevents our success, a bad self-image. You will not be able to rely on and trust yourself if you perceive yourself in a negative light. Eating healthier will help you fix that. You will begin to feel better about the choices you make. The nutrients you take in will help you feel energized and motivated; you will be ready to face those problems and that stress instead of trying to forget about it until it piles up on you. Your lethargy will be gone and will be replaced with a new sense of pride about yourself and the initiative to bring change. Not only should you be aware of the food you eat, and everything that enters your body, you also need to pay attention to your surrounding, that means who you hang out with.

How you feel about yourself also depends on what kind of people you surround yourself with. Spending more time among people who are negative or make you feel low and ugly will certainly make you like that. It is always good to be among chirpy and positive people who can boost your confidence. Don't dress the way the trend is at the moment, but choose something that will make you comfortable and look hot. Create you own style statement. It is necessary to spend time doing things that give you joy. This will make you feel happy from within and will automatically reflect on your face, making it glow. Thus, to enhance your looks it is necessary for you to look great from within. Learn to be approachable and open up with friends. Staying aloof will only make you go unnoticed. Develop confidence in your speech, walk, and everything that you do. To come across as appealing you need to love yourself, polish your personality, and be confident. Taking care of these things will make a tremendous positive change in your life. It's all about how you put your mind in the thinking process. Accepting the truth will only boost your self-esteem and thereby build your confidence level. Rather than possessing an egocentric outlook, it's good to accept the ground realities of your personality.

Instead of focusing more on your weaknesses, it is best to focus on your strengths and see how you can make them to work. Each individual has a distinctive quality that can make him/her stand apart in the crowd. You need to realize it and polish it to achieve your goals. Each achievement will boost your confidence urging you to do even better every time. Try loving yourself and feel good about what you are. Change the perception of life, which will help you progress and develop self-confidence. It is time to release the past, to give up that which no longer serves our development, and to reconstruct on a fresh foundation. We're all healers, and this is a good chance to transform our experiences in a way that will nurture our soul. We should not feel guilty for producing a life of happiness. There's no demand to harm those who have restricted us in freeing ourselves. And, in a few cases, we might have to break away from a vocation, a line of work, a relationship, or even loved ones in order to produce the life we wish. All the same, most letting go isn't typically burning up a bridge, but a great deal of the time letting go is an inwardly job: letting go may imply changing our belief formula, a way we work on emotion, or how we see life.

You have to have a mental attitude of Appreciation for the great things in your life while you're implementing the healing process. Don't center on simply the negative. It"s really hard to be depressed when you're calculating your blessings. Another thing that I've come to realistically believe is that there's so much fear that takes over our natural ability to overcome any obstacle in life, take for instance public speaking simply the act of talking in front of a group of people. The group can be quite small or impressively large. In either case, many individuals find the process to be overwhelming. Speaking in public is an art. Effective presentations require clear delivery that includes proper inflection, pauses and emphasis. Some people seem to have the knack for oral presentation while others struggle with this type of activity. Natural talent does help. However, effective public speaking can be achieved with research and diligent practice. The art of oral presentation is one that can be mastered with the right methods and persistence. This form of communication is also a science.Though the very thought of speaking in front of a crowd is overwhelming, it is important to take time to make a clear distinction between fears and phobias.

Chapter Nine: Mind Fear

You may find that you are more than simply afraid of the task. If you have a phobia then there are other precautions that you need to take. Fear can be such a prominent emotion that you may feel confused about possibly having a phobia. After delving into the similarities and differences you may come up with a valid conclusion on your own. You may also want to consult a professional if you feel that you truly do have a phobia. Fear is a fundamental emotion that serves a very important purpose. This particular emotion is designed for self preservation. Without fear, people may engage in activities that are far too dangerous. Survival of the human race would be at risk without this necessary emotive force. In spite of its fundamental nature fear is a very complex emotion that has several sources. This emotion is typically hardwired into our beings to ensure our safety. The severity of the apprehension and anxiety associated with the feeling varies from person to person. The body has a prominent response to this emotion. Physical changes occur in our bodies when we feel fear.

Trembling, tenseness and rapid breathing are common signs. Increased heart rate, sweating and dry mouth can also accompany this emotion. Blood flows away from the brain to other parts of the body since the energy can be better used to run or stand up to the challenge. The thought of speaking in front of so many people causes these very reacts. Just like fear hinders other aspects of our lives. It's something we must get past in order to live more abundantly. In order to overcome a fear, it is necessary to recognize the root causes of it. Fear is an important emotion that is designed to help us protect ourselves. Some emotions are hardwired into our system in order to keep us out of danger. Even the fear of public speaking may have roots in self preservation. Fears can also be learned. We can adopt a fear of a certain situation through our experiences. Some of us find ourselves fearful of an object or circumstance when we see others fearful of it. Of course, it is obvious that a person is not facing immediate threat of harm when he speaks in public. However, there are components to the emotion that are self-preserving in nature. Fear of public speaking is complex because it seems to be a combination of both instinct and learned fear. To what extent either has influence is unknown. Now you must realize this can't be done overnight. Changing your lifestyle requires dedication. When you feel good about yourself, you can then start to rely on yourself.

When going through our healing of wounds we likewise have an excellent chance to clear our inner 'file drawers' where aged, disregarded, buried matters are stored beside the fresh ones. These techniques are especially helpful in this respect, enabling us to decrease the strength of residual notions from old grief along with new, raw feelings from the fresh ones. We likewise learn compassion by our own experiences of sufferings. This is generally acknowledged in the observance that many of the better caregivers for ill people are themselves injured healers. Closure isn't a time or date when you shut the door on your wounded feelings and feel it no longer. Closure begins the instant you soak up the fact that the situation happened. With each step along the path of healing wounds you take is a step toward further, deeper closure. Several are led astray to feel they've reached an early end to to feel they've reached an early end to their closure when they're in the grasp of waves of sorrow, anger and shame of the moment. Learning that healing has its own method, its own timing and its own meandering, hilly road toward ever better closure is a part of the process. It's an awareness regarding the procedure of grieving and healing; a growing intimacy with how your mind and feelings react and deal with emotional wounds.

In this life there is transience in all experiences. Recognizing an end will bear on every and each relationship we have, including the elemental end of our relationship with all we have lived in this life, helps us to treasure every experience a great deal more. This awareness might be one of the biggest benefits of transitioning through the healing process. Once we come through such grave challenges, other issues in our life shrivel up in comparison. As we clean-cut issues and feelings in the present tense, we frequently discover like issues lurking in the same file drawers. These might have been stacked away many years before, at times when we didn't bear the resources to handle them. At present, with the successes of managing problems of grief and healing, you can do an exhaustive clearing up of such unnecessary baggage that you carry with you in your unconscious. This is the acceptance of grief as a part of healing; as that which bestows deep -meaning to life as a chance for clarifications; and as the terrific teacher it may be. We may than accept everything in our life as a lesson. Rather than saying, "Oh, my goodness! How will I handle this challenge?" we can state, "Hmmm! I"m curious what intriguing lessons I'll get from this invitation to look deeper inside myself?" or "I question what I'll discover to clear up next from the file drawer that this hurdle is directing me towards ?

Chapter Ten: Emotional /Mental Wounds

As grownups, we go on to stuff uncomfortable feelings within ourselves, closing a mental door to keep them safely away from our awareness. Our unconscious mind watchfully stands guard over these emotions shoved away in files in the caverns of our being, stands firm against releasing them still when we're no longer in the dreadful situations that caused them still when we're clearly in a more beneficial position to cope with them. Your negative, wounding memories can be transformed into profoundly healing and growth-enhancing experiences. While immersing these memories protects us as youngsters, this leaves us bearing a lot of buried 'material' that's stacked away in our unconscious and in our heart. Our unconscious youngster mind sets up platforms to prevent our being harmed by these hidden burdens: it leads us to stand back from anything similar to what we experienced lest we hurt again as we had hurt before. Our grownup experiences might leave us with damaging feelings likewise. We have all experienced things that we wish had never occurred.

When we grasp that things that we're feeling, trusting and behaving, it's really not that hard to make substantial shifts into better personal places. When we no longer anticipate rejection and failure, we're much less likely to act in ways that will bring us to that place which we fear. If we discover ourselves blocked in our advancement in life or in our enjoyment of life, be it in our personal, relational, professional or spiritual lives, taking a close look may help us to change our negative notions and expectations. This then lets us alter our associated feelings and behaviors and to remold our ways of relating to ourselves and other people. Always make sure to keep an eye on your attitude, for that's very essential to understanding how that affects your life and the way you view it. As people grow up seeing things around them, they can form attitudes based on what they see. What they see can affect their perception of a certain person, thing or idea. Attitudes are part of a person's personality and the well being of a person. Attitude is responsible for projecting a personality, be it positive or negative. Your personality can be a factor in determining a mental state of being and contributing to the aging process.

Your attitude can also be defined as a form of an egotistical state of mind, regardless of whether it's about acceptance, expression of control or other traits that are considered to be selfish in nature. If you are continuously angry and feel a hatred towards others, that can be described as having a negative attitude. These forms can affect how you think and act towards others. When you start having negative thoughts, you open yourself up to premature aging and possible health issues. It's very important that you steer clear from having a constant, negative mindset. Of course, this transformation takes time. After all, you didn't form these negative thoughts overnight. You have to work at making an honest effort to change your attitude and your outlook about things. If there were things that bothered you in the past, you have to release them and move forward. Being bitter will not help you; it will only accelerate the aging process and could also affect your health, physically and mentally. It's easier and healthier to look at the bright side of life. Doing this will refresh your mind and your body. Don't let things that are out of your control get you down. A lot of times, it may be out of your control. Don't be mean to people because they are mean to you. Being nice will help to maintain a positive attitude, no matter what the situation is. When you think negative, it can affect your mind and your spirit. Everyone in their lifetime has either said or thought something that did not line up with anything positive in their life. It seems as though people spend more time in pessimism than they do in optimism.

Some people tend to make negative thinking a part of their daily lives. There are obstacles that seem to block us from what we want to do. Instead of pushing those obstacles out of the way, some people find it easier to complain. They don't realize that it won't help the situation. They will still be stuck in the same place with no movement. You will continue to be stuck in the same place if you are a constant complainer. Everytime you complain, you take away a moment of happiness and fulfillment that you could have. Plus, other people don't care to be around chronic complainers. Think about what you are saying when you do that. You could be using your time doing things that will uplift you and keep you active. Before you know it, you'll be so involved in what you're doing you won't even think about complaining anymore. When you think negatively, you want everyone else to think the same way. People that think negatively often have imbedded bitterness because of things that happened to them in the past. They never got over the situation; it may have been from being passed over for a promotion; a boyfriend, girlfriend or spouse leaving them; or feeling rejected from a parent when they were little. Any of those scenarios can still up feelings of bitterness. Or they can be jealous of someone else that is doing better than them in things like losing weight, making more money or just being happy. They can't stand to see the other person happy and they continue to ingrain bitterness inside of their soul.

Bitterness can take a toll on a person's health. It can cause them to have wrinkles and create health issues, such as high blood pressure or cancer. If you need help releasing these bitter tendencies, it's best to seek counsel from a family member, or therapist. Otherwise you will look old before your time. You should not be thinking pessimistic thoughts. Pessimistic thoughts spread faster, like a virus. It's important to remain positive in the midst of what is going on in your life. You need to know that things in your life will work out for the best. You have to keep the mindset that you know things are going to work out for your good and in your favor. This is something a lot of us fail to do. People spend so much time worrying about things that are out of their control instead of focusing on things that are constructive. Some of the things are so simple, that you don't have to spend a lot of money doing them. Try taking a walk in the park or going to the library. You may want to take a writing class. You may think these are not the most exciting things to do, but when you think about it, they are constructive activities that can add to your well-being. It's good to have a few friends around to keep you company. You don't have to have an army full, just two or three is fine. Besides, if you had so many, how would you be able to keep up with them?

Living longer and staying young also depends on your circle of friends. They can't just be any friends. They must be people of substance, people that will be with you in good and bad times. They must be people that won't put you down when you make a mistake; instead they will lift you up with encouragement. It's usually better to stick with true friends than always commingling with relatives. There are times when relatives will try to undercut you just because you're related to them. They are also quicker to take advantage of you than your friends will. You real friends will genuinely care about you. They will make sure that you are taken care of and that your needs are met. However, keep in mind that friendships are not created overnight. You should have positive relationships with your friends. This is what will keep you going and not to stray into the aging process. When your friends are positive, then that positive vibe can rub off on you. You need friends to go out to dinner or a movie with just to have a good time. You can have a freedom with your friends that you may not have with your relatives. These relationships will make you feel vibrant and refreshed. You will have renewed energy in your life. You won't necessarily have to concern yourself with being stressed when you're with friends as opposed to relatives. Because your relatives are familiar with you, they think that they can run over you and treat you any way they want to.

Chapter Eleven: "I can't"

Thinking positively may sound like generic advice that has no value, but in fact, it is a critical component of success in our life, our personal relationships, and our work. Thinking positively shapes how you see the world, how you make decisions, and how you feel about those decisions at the end of the day. So, next time you start thinking "I can't do this," think again. Start with the premise that you can do it; and then figure out how. For instance, maybe you can't do the task by yourself, but if you ask for the help of others, you may find that the task is trivial. No matter what you do, don't give in to negativity. Thinking negatively will drain your motivation; and make it much harder to achieve your goals. In some situations, it makes sense to quit. For instance, if you are implementing a new marketing plan for your business; and it turns out to be enormously expensive and generates no profits, it may be a good idea to give up on it and try something else. In many, many other situations, however, we give up when there is no good reason to do so. Perhaps we're about to finish some very difficult task, but we run into an unusually long string of snags right before we complete it. As a result, we get so discouraged that we simply give up. Well, it's time to put an end to this. No matter how tired you are, no matter how discouraged you are, don't give up. If you can't finish something tonight, give yourself a break, and finish it up the following day.

Throughout our lives, we repeatedly hear that hard work is the key to success. But sometimes it isn't. In some cases, working harder and longer hours won't bring you closer to your goal; it will only move you further away from having perspective and it will only sap your energy further. So make sure you take breaks. Take some time to step away from your goal, rethink it, and decide whether it is truly something you want to accomplish. And, better yet, take some time to thing of other things, too. If you let your goal completely dominated all aspects of your life, you may find yourself drained and unable to continue. This shouldn't need to be said, but often it does: if you don't enjoy what you do on a regular basis, then you're going to have a very difficult time achieving your goals. The reason for this should be obvious: even if you "know" you should be working towards your goals, the pain and discomfort associated with them will push you too far in the opposite direction. This is why it is important to make sure that you enjoy your life, even as you work towards very difficult goals. You can start by revising your current approach to accomplishing your goals, so that they become more enjoyable. Another thing we often do is live in complete fear of failure. We spend so much time convincing ourselves that we cannot accomplish something (and that when we fail to accomplish it, our lives will be horrible) that we stop working towards it all together. Instead of trying to accomplish the goal; and being disappointed only if we fail, we convince ourselves to hedge against failure by only putting in half as much effort as we could.

Just like fear of rejection, fear of failure can be highly detrimental to our personal and business endeavors. One of the most destructive things you can do to your productivity and to your goals is to procrastinate. Of course, everyone knows this; and it is certainly simple to say and to understand, but doing something about it is an entirely different story. Day dreaming can go a long way in helping you to stay motivated. It can help you to visualize how you will feel and how your life will be tangibly different when you finally accomplish a goal. And from these day dreams, you can draw motivation to ensure that all of those things happen. With that said, it is important not to let day dreaming overshadow the deep, thoughtful, analytical thinking that is needed in order to actualize those goals. So let yourself dream and visualize, but also try to remain alert, focus, and ready to solve problems and tackle challenges.One of the things that prevents many people from succeeding is a fear of asking others for help. In most situations in life, there is someone other than us who knows better; and would be willing to help us if we'd only ask. But we don't ask them. Instead, we plod away endlessly, wasting time, and ultimately having nothing to show for it. Instead, I suggest that you push hard towards your goals, fail if you can't do them; and, then, after accepting failure, approach someone else for help. The first time you do this, you may find it is quite difficult. But after a while, you'll realize that it isn't as bad as what you were doing before: wasting endless amounts of time trying to do something that you didn't truly understand.

We all know how bad it is to build and reinforce bad habits. It can be as simple as trying something once, finding out you like it, and then continuing to do it on a regular basis, even if you know it's detrimental to your work schedule or personal life. One trick to getting motivated and achieving your goals is to do the opposite of this to build good habits, to reinforce them, and to allow those habits to govern your behavior on a daily basis. Of course, saying this is easier than doing it. All you have to do is find out when you work best or when you think clearest; and then reinforce habits that push you to work or think at those times. If you're like many people, you get as much information as you need to complete a task, and then you shut your brain off to new information. For instance, at work, you might be learning to use a new software program. As soon as you learn all the basic controls, you no longer feel motivated to continue to learn about it. This can be highly detrimental to success at work, as it can prevent you from truly mastering your surroundings and your tools. I personally suggest that you instead make an attempt to adopt a continuous learning model, where, each day, you make an effort to learn at least 1 new thing about your surroundings and your tools. Self-confidence is an important part of motivation. When you feel confident about your skills and abilities, you also feel confident that you can carry out the task at hand with some degree of success. To the contrary, when you lack confidence, it almost always translates into poorer performance. This is why it is so important to stay focused on your strengths, rather than your weaknesses.

If you do focus on your weaknesses, focus only on how you can eliminate them. But what is even better is if you focus mostly on your strengths; and think about how you can use them to your advantage, no matter what position you find yourself in. Some people and activities make you happy, bubbly, excited, and inspired. Others make you sad, tired, lethargic, depressed, and dispirited. It's important to realize who these activities and people are; and to choose your actions wisely as you encounter them. If certain people constantly drag you down, then you should make an effort to avoid them. And if certain activities drain your energy, but provide little to no return, then you should make an effort to avoid them, too. Overall, you should try to shift your activities and relationships, so that you spend more time on those that provide you with motivation; and help you to achieve your goals. Next time you're faced with a challenge that threatens to prevent you from accomplish a goal, don't back down or give up. Instead, dig in, think hard, and figure out how you can overcome this challenge. No matter how difficult it seems and no matter how poor your prospects of success seem, push forward until you overcome the challenge. Once you have overcome the challenge, celebrate it with your family and friends. Go somewhere special with your spouse or significant other. Take the night off from work. Do whatever it is that makes you happy; and will encourage you to continue to overcoming challenges in the future.

One of the most unproductive ways in which you can spend your time is to worry about things that might or might not happen. If they don't happen, then you wasted precious time worrying, rather than working. And if they do happen and couldn't have been prevented, then there's nothing you could have done, anyway, so your time was still wasted. Finally, if they happened and were preventable, then you should have spent your time figuring out how you could have prevented them from happening, rather than worrying. In short, whenever you're encountered with a problem, don't worry. Either fix the problem by taking steps or don't worry at all. Many of us fear rejection or failure even before we attempt to try. Failure is a part of life and one must experience it at least once. However, to fear will only take you away from success. In this competitive world, it is essential for one to overcome their fears and develop selfconfidence. Developing self-confidence may take some time, but it is not impossible to become a confident person. Self-confidence plays a key role in shaping our personality and future. No one is born perfect and all of us learn as we go through life. Some grasp things very fast, while some may take time. If one person is master in one field, another may be good in something else. We all have some skill that can take us ahead in life. We only need to realize it and nurture it accordingly.Never think negatively of yourself, this will lead to you being an emotional wreck, the best thing to do no matter how hard it is, is to be positive in all you think or do!

Chapter Twelve: Mental Loneliness

Some of us experience being alone, and leaving ourselves in idle, believing all types of things that are not true about ourselves. Maybe you are the kind of person that has given up on your dreams, and feel there too far out of reach. Is there something you always wanted to do, and have you to mustard up the strength and courage the reach a better part of yourself. Everyone in the world has felt this emotion one time or another. Especially in these times rapid technological growth the feeling of loneliness is rapidly increasing. Being alone does not equate to being lonely because sometimes it is good for a person to be alone and at times it could be very refreshing as the person has the opportunity to refresh, recuperate and rediscover part of our lives. There is no one in the entire universe that will have the same personality, ideas, way of life and needs like you.If you are mixing with a crowd that is negative and makes you feel down all the time, it is no surprise why you are lonely and negative. It is no surprise that children move out from their homes away from negative parents or stop interacting with certain groups of friends all together. Don't let the poison drain your energy. The feeling of loneliness is radically due to the failure of man in loving others. The symptoms of loneliness magnetize the effects of the pain to the extent that it forces the focus of attention more on ourselves and creates a self-preoccupation that creates an obstacle to love others.

Emotions can play tricks, therefore it is wise to observe and pay attention as you move along to command and master the emotions. This will help you spot tricks that come to the front, and will help you to work against the tricks the mind plays. Refining the mind toward a positive direction is the process of polishing and cultivating new habits, behaviors, and way of thinking. The process is a form of filtering the information you achieve and distill it to rid impurities. The process of sharpen the mind is great, and this process will include observation, a willingness to accept self and changes, alone with an ability to feel discomfort at times and realize it is ok to feel discomfort. The thing is you want to avoid chastising self and others unless you have valid purpose to do so. Thus, check your validity. It is important that you develop smoothly to command and master the emotions. On gloomy days, you may feel the world has you down. Your eyes may dangle, as you stare aimlessly in no apparent angle. The gloom may make you feel empty inside. The key is bringing self out of this mood, since it will only put the emotions in control otherwise, you will be fighting very hard against your own emotions. If you find it difficult to control your emotions you may want to sit down an examine self. Examining self will help you to see areas you can improve. If you have, fears learn to face those fears and move ahead. Now take some time to sit and think of what causes the emotions to control you.

We all have setbacks in life. Sometimes we go through trials and tribulations that make it next to impossible to get back up and fight. If you have a will and self-control however, you can get back up and start moving ahead. If you experience a death in the family, realize that everyone dies at one time or another and this is something you have no control over. It is not your fault, therefore pick up those spirits, and keep fighting to achieve and accomplish. Some days we feel miserable, which makes us feel lousy inside. We might stare upward at the air with the eyebrows raised and the mouth sagging. Some days we feel grumpy. We might lay our head down, droop the mouth and with eyes half closed, we might just think gloomy thoughts. At times, we may feel lonely. A lonely state of mind leads us to feeling alone. We may feel lost, lonesome, and feel like we don't have a friend in the world. We may feel deserted, abandoned, or simple secluded from the world. This brings in a forlorn feeling, which makes you feel sad. It is a pitiful look showing on your face with a despondent gaze. You feel hopeless and unhappy. What can you do? If you feel lonely, is it possible you can call friends? Do you have family that makes you feel good inside? Using your thinking cap can help you overcome many emotions that effect your life.

If you allow emotions to rule, you will find self-drooling often. A desperate mind creates intense emotions, thus trying to avoid desperation could be a way to learn how to master and control the emotions. Desperation only brings in extreme anxiety, worries, fear, anguish, and the like. A person often feels distracted and feels hopeless. If the mind is distracted it will experience interruptions, diversions, commotion and so forth. This too brings in anxiety and agitation. As you can see emotions that expose self-need someone to control them. If you do not gain control of your emotions, your emotions will control you and soon not everyone around you will like your company. The mind requires training to work sufficiently.To train the mind, you must understand that self-control, hope, confidence, self-esteem, self-assurance, and all those other words fit into the equation. The more you build on your human requirements, the higher the possibility you will grow toward mastering and commanding your emotions.As you see, alertness of the mind is essential while dealing with problems. If you are alert, you will have the ability to take control at what time control is needed. The mind response well to alertness and that awareness includes understanding what is inside of you. You will never know your limits until you take the steps to put action in full force. Now, pull out those dust cloths, Windex, and open the windows in your mind.Stop thinking low of yourself, you are loved and very special!

Everyone wants to live a life according to their dreams and wants; everyone wants to have a happy ever after ending. There will be such a time that you will feel that you are going on the wrong direction and that your life's journey is not where it should be. These times can be the coldest part of your life and you will suddenly feel that you need changes. But how can you change your life in an instant? Well, it is impossible especially if you don't know where to start the changes. As a person, you should know what you want to change in the different aspect of your life. Knowing this will definitely lead you to real and absolute happiness. Most people have more than one aspect in life that they would want to change. They want to improve self esteem, want to fix a relationship, lose weight, improve financial situation, and change other areas of their lives. Wanting to change is normal, it is definitely not unusual, but making a change is another story. But why do people can't quite actively work in changing and improving their lives? People can't change because, they don't exactly know how and if they already know how, they will find that trying to change is hard. There are some people who actually know how they can change their lives but they considered change as too difficult to achieve. Thus, some people don't want to try or they try but will eventually quit. The key to making a change in your life, once you learn what areas you want to change and know what to do to make this change, is to have a firm commitment and dedication to make changes.

However, the commitment is usually the hard part because if you are not entirely committed to change, you are likely to stop and quit every time you have some obstacles. Before changing your life, you must know what you really want. It's the best pursuit to happiness. If you don't know your ultimate dreams, how will you able to change your life? Well, it would seem impossible to pursue. Remember, everything you do in your life is a choice, and everything you don't do in your life is also a choice. The right mindset is the key to success. It will get you unstuck and will help you grow every day. In battling for you future, you need to have strategies that will help you get the perfect mindsets for success. Whatever your plans and goals in life are, you need to know that success is battles that are fought in your mind. If you believe doubts and hindrances, if you are focusing only to your failings, success will be impossible for you to achieve. It is time for you to make some action, take charge, and do it the right way to take the steps to achieve your goals. Set your mind and stay focus on the right path ahead! You need to set your mind and focus on your words to achieve the maximum benefits. Knowing yourself is the hardest part of all. It is easier to offer opinions to others about the different things, but if it is about you it will be a bit murky. It depends upon your self esteem; you can undervalue yourself or be so full of yourself without seeing the reality. Knowing who you really are, what motivate you, what your passion is, then you can start helping other people as well.

Chapter Thirteen: Affirmations Of The Mind

You're a human, this is a fact. You have those feelings that can change frequently. To have the right mindset, you can't afford living with your feelings. More often than not, feelings are unreliable and can also lead you away and astray disabling you from fulfilling your goals and complain about lots of things. Discover its real essence and benefits if you don't possess the right attitude towards these words. The brain is amazing in lots of ways, how it can process information and how it delivers your impressions and thoughts. Sometimes, however, your brain can also fail you. Challenge your assumptions, and replace them with evidences. Action is a powerful motivation that will help you keep going. It is better that you start on something and then adjust things as you go about rather to keep on planning, taking notes, but never taking them into action. Take action, it will make you feel great about yourself. Don't worry about mistakes that you might incur, pick yourself, readjust, and try again. Always aim forward. There are actually lots of ways that you can do to improve and develop yourself. Through both positive and negative mindset, you will be able to look for possible problems and then learn to appreciate all the things you have. People have thousands of thoughts every day, and these thoughts and their nature will make up someone's outlook in life. Both negative and positive are essential to the mind, but it is vital to use them properly.

As a person, you should learn the right way of using both negative and positive thinking. Both positive and negative thoughts can strengthen your self esteem, through everyday affirmations in order to help yourself realize your skills as well as your personal drawbacks.Identify your life's situations where you would want to change your negative thinking habit. Listen, attune, and continue the qualities that are emerging within yourself. A calm mind and sound body are the most essential elements to offer you calmness, peace. Positive affirmations are simply a self talk. This will help you reach whatsoever goals you have set for yourself. They may, in reality, switch your thoughts, resulting from that negative self talk to those more powerful positive thoughts. Consider your positive attributes. Scrutinize of yourself by making an inventory of your best qualities, abilities, or other attributes. Are you gorgeous? Put it down. Are you a hard worker? Make note of it. Write every quality down in a short sentence, beginning with "I" and utilizing the present tense: "I am beautiful," for instance, or "I'm generous". These statements are affirmations of who you are. We seldom center on those things that we truly like about ourselves, instead deciding to linger over things we'd like to change. An inventory will help you break that cycle, and utilizing these affirmations to help you appreciate who you are will present you the confidence you need to accept your affirmations of who you wish to be.

Positive affirmation or positive self-talk may benefit not only yourself but likewise other individuals that you interact with. Affirmation is the switching of thoughts resulting from damaging, dirty, and rough experiences or ideas to a more positive note. It relies on the principle that you may only become successful if you tell yourself "I can do that" rather than saying, "I can't do that." Positive affirmation brings to life an individual's capabilities, strengths, talents, and skills. Perpetually repeating the things that you're capable of doing and forgetting hesitant feelings that commonly hinder you from going after a certain goal may help a lot in accomplishing a positive result. A light outlook, a smiling face, and a worry-free aura are commonly the features of very successful individuals. The principle of positive affirmation leans on the core tenets that the mind is just so mighty and what it says is commonly followed and miraculously accomplished by the body. Our thoughts, self talk and affirmations, both positive and negative, get to be self-fulfilling prophesies much more often than not. Your actions and effort are influenced by what you're thinking, so if you think you'll fail at something you likely will. Likewise, if you think you'll succeed you likely will. Most individuals don't realize that it is actually possible to choose to more think more positively. The consequences of such a choice are that your consequences are truly the ones you consciously want.

In our daily lives we often face complexity, difficultness, pressure and other forms of stress, creating a wide array of anxiety. This has been a part of our routine each day as we wake up in the morning. We are so busy doing things that we forget how to find peace of mind to help us get relaxed and be calm as we indulge in the facets of our daily living. Looking for peace of mind is very hard because our mind is bombarded with negative thoughts, restless disturbing worries, that we cannot find the calmness we need that gives us freedom from fretfulness that eventually leads to a state of happiness, contentment and pleasure. What really hinders us from being calm and possessing the inner peace is excessive thinking of mistakes and pressures that may occurred in the past or we are enduring in the present situation. We can always plan for the future but we can still live the moment. Achieving this kind of serenity gives us the confidence and the clearer version of what we usually think, therefore, this allows us to prevent and put away anything that bounds our potentials and possibilities. This gives us the audacity and the ability to reflect comprehensibly. We all rush things up that we forsake the beauty of the present moment which is unfolding beyond our very eyes. We always anticipate the next problem or another great thing to happen. Upon realizing and accepting yourself and your being, now its time to open up your heart in terms of your relationships to your family and friends. Sometimes we find it cynical when we do things our own way, we try to bypass others just to accomplish desired goals, by that, it serves as a barricade towards the feelings of others.

Chapter Fourteen: What about The Children

Of course simply said, our child is a success if they grow to be healthy, happy and able to be independent of us. However for most of us, while we say that is all we want for our children, it's not all we expect from them. Take a moment to look at your own life/ How do you measure your own success? Is it through the type of possessions you own, the work you do, the way you life your life? Is it your relationships, your children? Think about what you feel is a success in your life and write them down. The amazing thing about parenting is that we teach our children even when we don't mean to. So that list of your own successes are important. It gives you a starting point of what your child is already learning form you about what is important in your life, and they will follow it. Once you have created your lists read over it once more and think about how you learnt those elements of success. Put them into groups emotional, spiritual, and physical and economics. This report will help look at all of these as a group, but it's important to consider them individually to begin with. We all have different areas that we consider are the moment important to measure our success in. For some finding one person to spend the rest of your life with, raising children together, maybe the pinnacle of your success. For another it maybe growing a business and becoming the CEO of a world wide organization, and for another it may be working with a group of people who need the services f someone committing a lifetime of free work alongside them. All of these are important.

All of them add to the world we live in. To create a successful child, we need first to recognize that success isn't just about being the richest child on the block. It's about awakening the inert dreams and hopes each one of our children hold inside their heart and bringing them to life. If we do this, then our children will succeed. While our children will copy us, and follow us, they are not carbon copies of us. Even if you've come from a long line of doctors, and you yourself are one, it doesn't mean your daughter is going to be the same. Once we have worked out how we measure success and what values we want to share with our children through our modeling of those measures, we then need to acknowledge they are a separate person from us, and still may go a completely different route. The precise nature of how they show their success isn't as important as how they carry out any task before them. To succeed children need to be able to work with a wide range of people (have good people management and leadership skills), to be able to identify a problem and then also have an idea of how they can go about solving it. This combination is a winning success formula suitable to a variety of ways your child may display their success. Children need our expectations and our ability to call out of them positive attributes, but they don't need us to carve out a specific future for them. They are able, even at a young age to do that themselves.

Most children who grow to be hugely successful had often almost dysfunctional upbringings. They may have lost a parent early on, lived in near poverty or just never fitted into school. There are many external factors that occur to our children that we have no control over. And these things, instead of being a negative influence, can turn around and become part of what creates success for them. Perfection is not required. Luxury is also not a necessary part of your child's success. Children who grow up in luxurious surrounds with all their physical needs met don't develop the hunger they need to g out and make it on their own. They have no need to- to all intents and purposes they've already got it. Some very wealthy people choose to raise their children very humbly and simply to encourage them to create their own path to success. If we provide our children with everything they need, and everything they want, they have no reason to solve the problem of how to get what they want. If we have a lot it feels natural to give to our children. However the best gift we can impart is the gift of developing their own resourcefulness. It's a little bit more of a long term thing, but it's a powerful gift to give. This is great news for those parents amongst us who worry about how a lack of finances can negatively impact their child. It doesn't need to. The saying necessity is the mother of invention is certainly true when it comes to our children developing creative and inquiring minds.

The path to our children's success begins right at the start. Our children are not born as an empty vessel, waiting to be filled. Each one already has some innate talents, a personality that will develop and grow. If you have more than one child, you'll know how amazing it is to watch both children grow up in the same environment but grow so differently, and respond to different things. While our child is not an empty vessel, they are a little like a sponge, absorbing both the good and bad that comes their way. It's our job to create an environment that gives them a strong foundation to build their success from. Of course each and every one of us can think of one famous, extraordinarily success person who can from such horror and heartbreak that we look at that and see that only people with a tortured home life have the ability to succeed. But for every story of horror, there are far more people who succeed from happy, settled and sorted homes- their stories just don't make quite as good a read! To start the foundations right, all children need an environment of good boundaries, routines, rules and responsibility. These words are often bandied about but the following is a basic rundown of how these work to created success. Creating good boundaries is important. As an adult we sometimes make conscious decisions to enlarge our boundaries, to allow people to walk over us a little, or sometimes we do the same to them, particularly in business. But well established boundaries help in all areas of our life from relationships to business. They help us to avoid addiction, and build positive, strong and effective relationships with others- all of which add to our success.

Chapter Fifteen:Controlling your anger

Irrespective how curious it might appear to other people, each individual's behavior adds up once you're able to see it through their eyes; through their experiences. It isn't unusual for people to mistake their models of the world for the true deal. It seems real clear to us what occurred. We don't commonly relax and think that as of the model I have of the world, I decided to focus on these details and to construe those details in this fashion which led me to this conclusion-We generally simply think it happened this way, why can't you see it my way? Feelings passing as truths occur once you cloud your thoughts with truth. The emotional brain makes up its mind about how we feel about matters before the thinking brain is even cognizant that something has occurred. You're able to see how this might lead us to trust our feelings. Frequently raging people feel so strongly that their rage is rationalized that they assume there's no other explanation for what has happened. Studies have demonstrated that people who do things that most of us would see as destructive or raging like gang members, spousal abusers and belligerent road ragers generally feel that their rage is justified normally by past or present conditions.

The key here is to recall that once we're under tension our emotions are more likely to regulate our thoughts than the other way around and therefore what we're thinking isn't always sensible or accurate. Ask yourself, is this a truth or merely a feeling? Treat feelings as a loved one, treasured, trusted but imperfect acquaintance. Pay attention to them and value them, but admit that they might be incorrect at times. Feelings might be colored by tiredness, pain, stress or chronic attitudes. If after quiet analysis your rage does seem justified, recall that you're able to be firm, resolute and in command of your responses - without hate or resentment. Overgeneralization is making up one's mind that your damaging experiences apply to all situations. If this is foul, everything is. Well, no it's merely one situation. Every state of affairs and every individual is different. Words like always, never, everyone, nobody, all or none are suggestive of overgeneralization. some Ask if a damaging event might be an exception to the rule. Some people over generalize in the positive direction. Mad people live with elevated levels of frustration, but great angriness management methods let them learn to keep their irritation in check, by accepting their temperament, and accepting the responsibility of coping with it, by studying anger management techniques to deal with the prompts and triggers that might rapidly turn to angriness.

By exercising stress management techniques on a regular basis, and using physical exertion to work off their aggravation, they're able to realize the first signs of angriness, and take a time out to chill out, minimizing the likelihood of discharging their angriness on others. Mature people attempt to exercise positive ways to deal with their angriness in a controversy. One favorable way to cope with angriness against loved ones is to make a contract that they may leave during a riff, whenever they feel that they might lose control. Simply go to a private spot for break. Privately they perform damage control methods like waiting out the initial surge of the angriness, and attempting to think from the other individual's viewpoint, to bring their angriness level downward and then return to cope with the issue. Admitting that you've an angriness prone personality and recognizing the need to actively work towards angriness management in order to live a happier life, makes the difference in dealing with angriness successfully. A dedication to discipline and taking parenting classes to seek more efficient means of disciplining their children, taking angriness management classes, and taking part in couples counseling, helps mad people to learn more advantageous ways of being with the people they work and live with. A few people with high degrees of frustration monitor themselves and work at bringing down their angriness reactions, through positive angriness management techniques; as their moral sense tells them that their flare-ups harm others.

A few people realize that they're acting out mad reactions they learned from their own parents, and sending that legacy down to their own youngsters. A few get help as their mate gives them the ultimatum of threatening to leave them if they don't get help. A few get help only after they lose their mate and loved ones, but unhappily, a few never learn angriness management techniques that may save their relationships, if not their own lives. The beginning and most primary way to avail anger management help is to open up and express mad emotions and feelings that bring pain, stress and anxiety in a person with a sympathizing acquaintance or loved ones as most mad people require a kind ear when dealing with difficult situations. A mature listener will help the mad person comprehend the other person's point of view without wounding their feelings and smooth over rough spots in a calm manner, but sharing the issue is crucial to getting the correct help. Putting down mad sentiments or maintaining a journal is different effective anger management tip that minimizes tension as instead of speaking mad emotions, one has put them to paper; at times, this strategy is more beneficial than confrontation, which might bring conflict and rifts to further the problem if the person involved is likewise hotheaded.

Writing down mad feelings also has the advantage of being a technique that helps one make conclusions about trigger-factors that contributed to the person getting mad. On contemplation at a later stage one is able to re-read the notes made and this supplies insightful info on reasons for anger and maybe a clue into the true cause of the disruptive state of affairs. Discovering a solution is easier then, also. Staying away from a tense situation or going off on a vacation or even a walk (me-time) is a different way to cope with anger that cuts back tension and keeps a person away from possibly detrimental (for mental health) spots in addition to giving them time to contemplate their actions and the incident. Spiritual study, prayer, meditation, and stillness are additional procedures to deal with anger that bring down tension levels and wash off the pressures of life; people may take these up who are at ease with being solitary and wish to cause a positive change in their lives. They're likewise regarded as being a balm for broken spirits and corrective power for world-weary souls. Staying healthy and in shape, learning breathing and exercises, getting enough rest and communing with nature in addition to looking on the brighter side of life are a few other great ways to cope with anger and a lot of people find the answer in music as well as opposed to confrontational techniques. Select the one that fits you!

Once we think of anger we commonly think of the actions we see on the surface for instance, your body tenses, you may shout, throw things or get violent. All the same, this is really more of a definition of rage than anger. Anger and rage is not the same thing. You are able to be angry without being in a rage. Reviewing your own experiences you'll without doubt discover times where you got angry and dealt with it in an unaggressive way (e.g. Refusing the urge to hit your boss as you'd lose your job). Anger is an emotion that's normal to all of us. Commonly, it's an alarm that something is wrong. Utilize that signal the correct way and it may be your friend. Utilize it the improper way and its trouble. It's good to release anger. It takes an tremendous amount of energy to hold rage inside and it may eventually lead to hypertension, diabetes, gastric reflux, heart condition, cancer and a whole cluster of additional things you likely don't wish to have. Trust it or not, if you utilize anger properly, you might find that you have happier and fitter relationships. Positive utilization of anger may likewise build self-respect. If you're able to tell somebody your feelings rather than holding them inside. An illustration of a positive expression of anger may be that you've a friend that is perpetually late. This is really troubling to you, but you do say anything? If you don't one of two matters will likely occur. You'll either stuff and stuff and stuff till you explode at her or you'll begin to become passive aggressive and start to make excuses to avoid her. Either way you might lose a friend.

On the other hand, If you're able to tell your friend that being tardy is hard for you and makes you feel insignificant, she might really listen, apologize, and start to arrive promptly. You might really wind up closer than you were to begin with. The issue for many individuals in dealing with rage is that your habit (and its truly crucial to consider rage as a habit as that's all it truly is) is to drive right into the aggression acres. Your goal isn't to make anger disappear. Rather your goal here is to learn to deal with rage in different ways; ways that will leave you empowered rather than with the temporary fantasy of power that aggressiveness might give you. The choice of how you respond to individuals or situations lies inside you . If your rage really was effective individuals or situations would change and we wouldn't keep becoming irritated at them. You can't control others, the only thing that you are able to control is how you deal with and express your rage. In my experience, rage is almost like an addiction in that individuals are really creative in discovering all sorts of rationales for their rage. From time to time it's almost as though they're in denial. Part of the reason for this is that they way our conduct appears on the inside may look a whole lot different to somebody on the receiving end of things!

Chapter Sixteen: Learning to have Gratitude

Why can't you be more grateful? It's likely at some point you've heard this remark from a parent, grandparent or have even uttered these words to a child yourself. (Or even worse, a partner!) Our need to see gratitude in others is a huge part of us seeing that person also as a loving, caring person. Having gratitude helps us to enjoy life more. It can break through huge barriers and reduce our stress loads, give us more confidence and help us to meet our goals- no matter how big they may be. There is now doubt that being grateful goes a long way. It's just how to be grateful in times of stress or when suffering from disappointment or sadness that's difficult. If you are struggling to find anything to be grateful for at all, start with your breath. It gives us oxygen, our chief nutrient for our body. Without it we cannot survive. It reminds us we are alive. And that alone is an outstanding thing to be thankful for. The drive to survive is far stronger than anything else. Your world may be crashing down around you, with creditors calling, relationships failing, and stress overload. But if you have breath, if you are alive, you are at a point where you can overturn all of that and start again. Try the exercise again. Do it several times in a row, taking in slow breaths then releasing it slowly with that pause in the middle. Try it with your eyes closed and let it still you. Gratitude can change our lives hugely. But first we need to take a look at where we are right now. In fact we possibly need to do a little navel gazing, and let it all hang out a little.

Often we are not honest about what parts of life we don't feel grateful in. We know we're meant to be thankful and we don't want to admit that we're not. It all feels a little naughty. So spend some time taking a little look inside your life over a range of areas. What on earth has happened to our manners lately? Please and thank you go further than ever before, simply because no one else is using them! It's true and fairly sad in many ways. If you are a parent one of the most powerful things you can do is teach your children to use manners. And it's not only the words it's the voice behind them. Parents often will tell a child to say it like they mean it. We as adults are no different. Use manners, and your world begins to open up socially. People watch us all the time as we engage with others. Gratitude is a way to showing respect to other people. Think about the last time someone said thank you to you and you knew they meant it. It does something quite magical to your relationship with them. Someone who honors what you've given them or some work you've done. If they thank you for it, the first reaction is often to want to give them more. Because you know that what you give them will be rewarded again- or at least you hope it will be! If we start thanking people around us for doing their job, for being kind, for giving us something when they don't have to, then it makes everything run smoother. People gravitate towards people they think are going to reward them for their actions. A smile goes a big way too. Smiling is an easy way to say thanks. If it's all you can manage, try a smile on a stranger today. They are likely to pass it right on to someone else.

It's a bit of a coarse way of thinking about it, but if you really can't think of any reason you should be grateful for people who are just doing what they are supposed to do, think of it as if you are just greasing the wheels. What that means is think about how easier it gets when you just give people a bit of your thanks. Sure, they may only be doing their job, but it's far better than all those people who aren't quite doing even that right? Thank people for the work they do, for any small kindness that comes your way and see how effective it is. Being thankful is the best thing in life, no matter what your going through. Once we are used to thanking the people around us, it's time to start being grateful for some of the good things working in our lives. This can be difficult to quantify, especially if you are under a fair amount of stress or finding life a bit tough. However there are so many things we have around us we take for granted, and often have no idea of the positive impact those things have on us. As is true with human nature, there are so many things we don't realize the worth of until we don't have around us. If you have children, you'll be aware of that sense of wanting your child to be asleep just so you can get something don't without them interrupting you, then when three are asleep, wanting them to wake up so you can hold them, touch them and play with them.

Or maybe you just have forgotten what it's like to live in your own place, without having your parents around to check what time you get home, or what it feels like to be able to drive somewhere, or go get a take away instead of cook. There are just so many little freedoms we have that we take for granted. Find things to be grateful for. Do you have any money on you at all? Be thankful even if it is merely a few coins. These are all small points of gratitude. This isn't about trying to find large big things to be thankful for, but together a little gratitude over a range of different things starts to add up. If you make this part of your everyday habits, along with getting dressed, eating, drinking and all those other important tasks then you start to focus on only what is positive and good. Doing this doesn't make the bad parts of our lives magically disappear but it does give us strength to cope with those aspects. If you are generally optimistic by nature, this can be enough to boost your optimism and keep you from stress. If you are naturally pessimistic, then this can help you move out of negative thinking and into something more uplifting. It's so hard to be happy if we can't find anything to be happy about. But spending time being grateful everyday helps us to naturally become happier. It makes our happy state less up and down and far more stable. This improved state of thinking provides a raft of benefits from increased confidence, to decreased ill health, to increasing our enjoyment levels across the board in a range of different situations.

The key is to do this enough that it slips into our sub consciousness. It's said that around ninety percent of our behavior stems from our subconscious self. How powerful is it then when we begin to act out of gratitude rather than defensiveness or negativity? It also becomes a self fulfilling prophecy. As we become happier, we naturally gravitate to things, people and situations that make us happier. In doing so, we begin to create a life that is all we desire and more. It's the true power of being filled with gratitude. So we've got the people around us feeling a little happier and our minds getting the happy message abut what about our bodies? What does being grateful do to our body? Our cells are constantly changing, renewing and mending themselves. Many doctors recognize the worth in a positive attitude towards health In fact, if we feel good about ourselves we tend to look after our physical selves better. We make better food choices, eat for hunger and not to stave off sad or complicated emotions and we enjoy making our bodies move. A happy body is a healthy body. Many obesity theorists think that one of the reasons that people in poorer areas are more likely to be obese isn't because they can't afford the right food, but that their misery at having no money, and limited resources impacts their emotions and drives their body to satisfy that need with food. And it's often over processed, sugary, body hating food they crave.

If your body isn't what it "should" be right now, or rather, if your body isn't want you want it to be right now, instead of focusing on the flabby bits, the sore bits, the needing to be operated bits, focus on the parts that do work well. One of the fascinating think about people who suffer from some sort of impairment is their body makes up for it in some other way. For example a blind person often has a highly developed sense of smell or incredible hearing. That is our body's way of being thankful for what does work. It compensates and provides an enhanced talent at the cost of the one the person doesn't have. For those raised in a home where faith was part of their lifestyle, the concept of thankfulness and gratitude is a big part of their culture. You may have been raised to give thanks before eating, or to say thank you to your god before bedtime. Once of the universal concepts is that we all need to be filled with gratitude in part because it is part of what makes the world go around. On the metaphysical level this is referred to as the law of Gratitude. This means that the universe, or the essence of life around us reacts to the thankfulness and it creates energy around us that impacts us and the people around us. As we are grateful, the universe responds by giving us what we are grateful for. This is the basic precept in the Law of Attraction that says the things we focus on are the things we attract more of into our life. The things you hold dear are the things you put your energy behind. The more energy we have around something, the more energy it attracts.

It's basic physics. So the things you may be grateful for- your friendships, your work, your health, your loved ones, grow and respond to that gratefulness the more and more grateful you are. Take a look at what you say and do. The person with a lot of gratitude in their heart speaks works of gravitates and attracts people around them that do the same. An army of positive people can't be all that bad! So we've covered all the good bits of our life and we're focusing on them. But what about the bad things that happen? Should we be grateful for them as well? Well yes, it's possible.Being grateful for bad things that happen to us isn't saying that what happened should have happened. It's not about lying down like a doormat; ready for the next punch life might throw at us. Being grateful about the bad things that happen is more about learning to live with the life you've had, and seeing the good that can spring from anything. If you look at people who are successful, often they have a tale of woe of how they struggled, were hurt, abused or injured. But somehow they rose above that and keep on going. Key to this and to their success was to not see their situation as something that broke them, but as something that made them. Being grateful for hardship. This doesn't mean that the universe is going to give you more if it. It's more of a letting go. You can have two people in life experience exactly the same turn of unfortunate events and manage it completely differently. hand of others is the one who is going to be positively affected by having gratitude in their life.

Being able to forgive someone for any wrongs done to you isn't so much about whether what they did was right or wrong, or even if they ever appreciate that you've forgiven them. Forgiveness is about what happens to your own heart during the process. As you forgive for the horrible parts of your life- forgiving a person, an object, a situation, the universe, yourself, you let go of the negative power that has over you and you can start to be thankful for the person you are now from that experience or event. It can be tempting to live in the life of what could have been. However this just leads to a stronger sense of loss and hurt and it's very difficult to move on from. If instead you focus on how it's shaped you, and given you a different perspective others may never get to see, then you start to take on a more positive slant. When bad things happen to us we all need recovery time. We need to look after ourselves and be gentle on our tender parts. But we can also look at the scars we carry and see them as little reminders of how we have survived. Battle worn some of us may be, but how awesome to have made it through to the other side. Learning from our experiences, and our past unwise decisions is about being grateful that you don't need to repeat the lesson again. You learn to read situations that others may miss, you can see things as they are, not as people try to portray them, and you change the way you see the world. When we are in the midst of trials and horrible experiences we often feel "What on earth that is good come from this situation. It feels like a hopeless case.

We wonder why we've got the feelings we do, know the people we spend time with, why doors aren't opening. It's often only with the benefit of hindsight, when we can look back and see how those times were the very ones that shaped us that we can see it was all worth it in the end. Often the very things we long for and want are not in the shape we expect. To get to those things we often have to go on a journey that we don't expect and experience things we weren't prepared for. To make us ready for the big dreams in our heart sometimes we get put into places and situations that build our mind and heart muscles. It might be loss, hardship, pain, death of a loved one. All to build us into the person we need to be to reach our dreams. Look at it this way. Imagine your dream is to own a mansion by the beach. If you don't have the character you need to won it, it won't be a lasting pleasure. You'll let it run down, or worse, you'll lose it. But if you are able to let like create the character in you that means you could look after it, well that would be worth it right? Sometimes our hearts need to tear a little, build a little muscle and then get a little stronger to reach our goals. If you learn the lesson fast, there is no reason for the bad even to repeats itself. While we never stop learning, and never stop experiencing life, as we learn from each one, the less difficult it is to learn from the next lesson. It's a bit like those muscles the more you use them, the more second nature it is to keep on building them and using them every day. The heart that is torn then built stronger finds it easier to be grateful, and tends to attract more and more experiences to be easily grateful for.

Chapter Seventeen: Innovative Thinking

Try a couple of the positive stimuli. This will be simple at first, but your ideas will dry out up. The magic is to continue; most of my finest ideas come up after a few days. Other instruments you are able to try to apply are mind mapping or associative thinking. They're pretty interchangeable. They merely refer to expounding ideas. Let's say you require themes for your fiction novel. Put down the name of the chief character and put a circle around it. Then branch off it with as many matters that pop into your head as you are able to. Offset circles may include painfulness, felicity, or even random matters like the moon, or a mint. Extend each of those circles. Painfulness may link to a different characters name, and then you may think up a dandy storyline involving treason by that character. All matters, from the invention of writing to the invention of the Net happened because of the practice of creative imagination. Synthetic imagination simply, at best, can improve upon what already lives. The adding of fresh things into being requires the use of creative imagination. The origination of wealth can be incurred, with diligence, through the informed and pragmatic use of synthetic imagination,However most wealth and most forward motion in human applied science happens through the use of creative imagination. Compactly put, your imagination is the workshop in which you, by and large without conscious acknowledgement, create the results that surface in your life. What you bear as an image in your brain is what turns up in your life.

If what you're imagining is merely a rehash of what has already happened or been produced by other people, then your results shall be limited to what has been, not what can be. The pitiful, sad, distressing thing that we impose upon our youngsters and ourselves is the stifling of imagination. Is the basic refrain. We neglect telling them or reinforce their personal self help and, help them comprehend, that all great and fantastic things that live in our world, had their genesis 'only in imagination'. As business minded persons, we became so highly skilled and adept in acting from the left side (the analytical, logical) of our brain, that we may be in peril of under using our right side (the artistic, intuitive) part of our brain. That's why scientists today agree that the roles and obligations of the brain can't be merely carved up as left-or right brain. Creative or artistic Imagination. When we get some "inspiration" and "intuitions", it's through the faculties of our creative vision that carry them out. This creative or artistic mental faculty becomes more mentally amenable and alert in relation to its evolution through constant use and practice. It mechanically works when our conscious mind acts at an extremely fast-moving rate and when it's excited through the feeling or emotion of strong want. By utilizing this creative imagination, leaders and groundbreakers in finance, business, and industry in addition to famous and notable poets, artists, musicians and authors become great and enormously successful.

Synthetic Imagination-this specific inborn power of one's mind works with the stuff of observation, experience and training, with which it's being fed. It simply classifies and arranges prior technique and expertise: thoughts, plan or concepts into new and new combinations. It's utilized by many groundbreaking thinkers and inventors whereas the genius draws on the innovativeness on the creative imaginative side where it can't solve problems by the synthetic imagination. So long ago, we were more intuitive and more effusive, but as we Understand and learned to use different instruments, and to convey verbally, we altered our state. All of us need to do to bring out and research our own creativity and accomplish maximum advantage from our innovative views is to be "whole-brain" thinkers. We heightened and advanced into a "left-brain" society by utilizing logic, verbalism and problem solving in a pragmatic manner. To be more expert and highly skilled in the building and stretching of our whole imagination and particularly our ingeniousness in the creative side, the primary key is in cultivating the right-brain function-our spontaneous emotions and our very own intuition. Only then we would be more all-around in our approach to business and life and consequently gain the supplied bonus that only our creative imagination can supply. In order to produce something for yourself, you have to resolve that what you want is yours today, not a week from now, a month from now, 5 years from now. Assume the feeling place of what it feels like to have or be what you wish, and then make the essential alterations in your life to produce it.

This may be uncomfortable from time to time and you might be stepping outside of your comfort zone, but by maintaining the vision of what you wish, you get clearer, and you establish your decisions based on your vision. Consider making your decisions from an area of already having what you wish, not from where you are today. Determine to keep stepping into your "yes." We live in an abundant existence and there's enough of everything for everybody. Everything we may potentially need or want is available to us, if only we let it into our experience. You can't evidence abundance with a scarcity mentality. Expect abundance in your life and let yourself receive it on all levels spectral, emotional and physical. Why do you wish what you wish? Tap into your life's role and your passion. Once you've placed what your passion and role are, it becomes easier to adjust with living authentically to let your life reflect that purpose in all facets. When you think about why you want something, your vibe usually shifts toward your want. If you consider how it will happen, or when, or who will bring it to you, your vibe generally shifts back toward the trouble and all the reasons why you can't have it. By applying all of these habits in your life, you'll discover your energy shifting. If applying all of them at once feels too consuming, start with one new habit at a time. Individuals will ask you what you're doing differently, what your "mystery" is. Your life will flourish.All of us tend to get bound in certain thinking conventions. Breaking these thought conventions can help you get your mind unstuck and yield fresh ideas.

Chapter Eighteen: Check the Nature of Attitude

Procrastination can be an enormous problem. In themodern world, when we all have so many things todo, it is increasingly important to know how tomanage our time and our life management. What really helps is learning to manage the emotionalreaction we have when we need to do something we don't want to do, don't like to do, or areconvinced we just can't do. Learn to understand why we avoid something, and it is a great deal easier to find a way to deal with it.There are many reasons why people procrastinate. Sometimes we put things off because we just don't like doing them. Sometimes we don't do something because we think we can't actually do it. Often we don't start something because we don't think we can do it well enough. For some people, there is a deep rooted psychological reason for not doing things. For others, it can just be a question of realizing that you don't enjoy doing something, or really dislike doing something. It is important to find out our own reasoning for putting things off, as this is the best way to devise methods of overcoming the problems of procrastination. There are all sorts of ways in which we can overcome procrastination. Not addressing the problem can be very life damaging. Procrastination can easily become habit forming, and can have a serious impact on our life, the lives of the people around us, and ultimately our health, both physical and mental.

For most people, it is a question of establishing that there are underlying emotional links between the tasks we put off and our inability to deal with them. So spending some time seriously questioning our feelings, as well as our actions, is really helpful. We also need to recognize that only Superman is likely to both enjoy and be good at everything. It is not to our detriment that we are not good at everything. Our self esteem does not need to be given a hammering if we accept that we have aspects of life that we are not good at, or just plain don't like dealing with. If you know you are not particularly good at organizing the finances, and accept that, you are more likely to be able to convince yourself that you should spend an hour or two dealing with the bank statements etc, than to spend it worrying that you won't be able to make the figures balance. Take the emotion and the fear out of the equation, and suddenly it's a whole lot easier. When you suddenly feel that sinking sensation, don't get up and find something else to do. Stop, and think about why it is you need to do this particular job. Think about the fact that, in deciding to do the job, you are doing something that will improve your life and something that is definitely in your best interests. The worst thing you can do if you are a procrastinator is to do nothing. The best thing is to begin by putting some effort into understanding why you do it, and by establishing some fairly straightforward organizational rules about how to use your time.

For most of us, there will be one or two things, at least, that we will put off dealing with. It is quite normal to procrastinate over something or other. For most of us, the problem is not too great, and doesn't threaten to destroy the quality of our lives. So time management, time boxing, etc is the way to deal with getting things back on track. Find a time each day when you will deal with something that you know you don't want to do. Give yourself a pat on the back when you have put in the time even if you haven't finished the job completely. What you have achieved is important you have made a start, and you have not run away from it. However, for some people, procrastination is a much more serious problem. For some people, there are deep seeded reasons for putting things off, or just not dealing with things at all! Some people have a subconscious reaction resulting from over controlling parents perhaps. Some have a deep rooted fear of failure, which has led to a resistance when dealing with certain tasks. Some people are frightened of not doing something perfectly. It might be painful to establish the reasons why we procrastinate, but it will certainly help to spend some time thinking it through. There are lots of fairly straightforward ways of helping ourselves improve our ability to deal with the million and one things that need to be done to keep our lives on track, and still have time to enjoy our leisure. Getting to grips with the idea that better time management, better task management and better self management is really about getting the best out of life. Wasting time is really not in our best interests.

Making time for enjoyment is!! There is a significant link between procrastination and perfectionism. Some people are frightened that they may not do something perfectly, and if they think they can't do it perfectly, they don't want to do it at all. Studies about perfectionism and procrastination vary in their arguments about the links between the two. Some indicate that striving for perfection is a positive thing. Others indicate that the desire to do everything perfectly is linked with strong need for order, tidiness, neatness, cleanliness, and generally very high standards that can become obsessive. Some studies link the intense desire for perfection with depression, and even suicide. There are studies that indicate that high achievers are perfectionists, and that even very successful people can have a propensity towards procrastination. How can one be a procrastinator and a highly successful person? Possibly one can achieve great success in one field, but at the expense of success in other aspects of our lives. Being driven by work can mean having little time or energy to deal with other areas of life. If someone else is always responsible for all the 'other' aspects of life, you don't get to build up the experience that means you know how to deal with them. Eventually they can appear too difficult to even contemplate. Managing life in this way can be done by having other people take responsibility for those aspects of our lives that we find we don't have time for. Perhaps areas of our lives that we just don't feel equipped to deal with, or uncertain about.

At what time negative influences come along put up your blocks rather than allowing them to hold you back from success. If you continue to explore the influences of your past, tear down the bridges and put up barriers to stop other negative influences in, you can succeed. Success is a state of mind also. When you tell yourself that you can succeed, likely you will go far. Become your own positive influence. Do your difficult tasks a part of bureaucratic sure not to lose one's temper when you undertake and you will find your efforts was worth it at the greatest end of your journey. Set your values, principles and affirm your beliefs so you can unlock your mind power to attract success, money and friends. The latent or subconscious mind setups selfish schooling below its absent-minded main course, explore this area. Subliminal self-mail are diversities of tack that we can relate to refer to as up that casual recollection down from the verge. We have collectible parts of our history at the lowest of the downward sensibility or subliminal mind that leeway our power. If we learn a scant knock off to exercise our empower alphabet to our message service, conceivable we can retrain the mind to enveloping mercy.

We have interpolated online mail in the subconscious or subconscious mind. We use these sources to make our continuous schoolhouse of knowledge engineer toward success. This gross bear of neural networks you intellectualize you have prior, is not gone, more agreeably, it is hermetical underneath the acquainted case satisfyingly for you to take an adventure to generate like now specifics to take steps to unlock the mind's power. You can unlock this power by confederating the integral nouns, such as objects, persons, knowledge, etc to attain what you had brain beforehand. You may memory duplexes as an urchin. A discussion you can relate to discover new faith moreover information that decide on service you to learn what you then fraternize by unlocking your backbone mind. You may recollection things that you did not flash on at this time, omnipresent you had to generate your subconscious mind into recalling. Yet as you put up and down the effort, you order on time grasp something you needed to do dozing in your soul mind. Likewise, if you take a ramble retract you can embark on to anamnesis cold fact of some advents that took place in your yesterday. For object lesson yesterday, your percipient mind exert jolt you to take a ramble repulse to records your knowledge engineering including succeeding your indispensable duty that could afford you.

Year-end step you take in hind part consideration you close in culmination to recalling, since your subconscious mind is improving. You may launch on reminiscence by associating occasion with your pivotal moreover low also fracture everyplace; you achieve what you have failed to memory in front. By implication objects, humankind, and machine learning from to remember you needed to do put away in the intuitive mind you start to anamnesis more anniversary daytime. You may have some remembrance of some anamnesis scarcely you id est. a juvenile. The priming explore maintenances you to come at new philosophy including intelligence that give the has an effect on of relief pitcher, since you embark to extract from today memories, thenceforth unlocking your hidden mind and breakthrough new methods and resources to better your life span. Each year you have to take it one-step at a time to make the steps come in union from one side to the other you take you be handy, summation to intelligent methods and means to make petty cash, or else to reach new humankind. Why, forasmuch as when the mood strikes you make pin money, common people generally breeze in* with the package, which in some events you decree make new come together.

Anybody You have to take it one step at a time to make the steps come in union from one side to the other you take excitingly retire in to your bygone times, you roll in epilogue to mending your mind's eye. To unlock this mind pleasantly however, you should want train every year dawn-to-dark. Train to resolve and cure you. Extract more knowledge engineering from your inmost, which you can put forth to your comfort. Activate your mind. To activate your mind, you have to extract from your inner resources. The most useful method to handle anything is by locating midget values to set about including labor toward broader morals following. You want to size your shrunk ideals into your overlong-language missions. Entrench your plans to labor in kinship with your ideals and work in harmony. easier. Sometimes you have to take excitingly receding steps in to your bygone times. You may have to go back where you originate concluded to mend your mind's eye. To unlock this mind accurately forever, you will need to oblige your mind's need and build up year-end sunshine as your work in harmony.

Tune up by ruling your support. Since you bring out more natural language processing from your essence, which you can bestow to your excellence, concentrate on your subliminal mind. Here you will find many answers. This is part of the experience of unlocking your mind's power. Year-end will step you up to take you to move to brighter ways to make pocket money, or else to meet a new nation of people. Pending on and off you will make small change, friends frequently fall by with this package, which in some causal nexus you decide on make new tie in.In short, when you find success, money follows and friends come behind success and money. You want to choose good friends. Positive friends that offer you something is the type of friends you want to meet. You may set sail on anamnesis by associating state with your centrals. The low moreover fracture in everything, you take each step with what you have.

Chapter Nineteen:Altering your Mind-training:

By implication items, bodies, including knowledge engineering from your history, you had put away in the mental mind you undertake to extract additional memories. You may have some recognition of some specific fluctuating you as it were a squirt. The directions explore assists you to find new tenets moreover guidance that give the has an effect on of relax, since you approach to extract from momentarily memories, hence unlocking your latent mind together with leap new methods and resources to better your future. You have to step deep in your subliminal mind and explore it willingly. If you do not have the willingness to learn what you already know, then you will only slow your progress to unlock your mind power to attract success, money and friends. Likewise, if you take a ramble to withdraw, you can commence to anamnesis the heart of some advents that took insert in your history. For case in point of the old days, your percipient mind will ordain to bounce you to take a stroll retire to records to your knowledge stored in your subliminal mind and houses the data you need to succeed your indispensable piece that could suit you.

Continue to challenge this subliminal mind to find what you know. To activate your subliminal mind, you have to extract from your inner resources. Take the challenge now so that you unlock your mind power quickly. Think of your challenges as something you want to master. Keep this in mind and you will go far. Discover your self-assurance. The Under consciousness science is the experience of comprehending happiness along with long-standing make-peace inside the boundaries of you by inspiring your mind to handwork in invitation with your body. Essence literature correctives you to fit the individual you want to polish. Under consciousness research supplies you to return on constructive thinking by dealing in to pick up your retrospection also to cultivate your organic inside. At what time an individual's taction wear down, they normally embark on to speculate detrimental double take from the subliminal mind. This causes befuddling. It brings into question. Essentially nature wisdom teaches you to flip-flop those partial disillusion to night shift an effective eccentric by engaging in meditation, or other alternatives.

Pondering can boost you with climbing your truthful being together with assist with self-sufficing tighten. In addition, subliminal schooling suffers of moving requiescence that you request in being.'Subconscious literature applies PC software that gives you systems theory hardware furthermore can hand you with tools to advancement peril of wellness program including to renew your take in of hang. This is the latest self-assurance-conformance preferences. The software programs bring about make on hand to you programs that make ready your mortal furthermore mind to take console. Essential nature study teaches you to exchange those colored rethinking to graveyard shift a constructive eccentric by engaged from contemplation, or other alternatives. Contemplation can furtherance you with soaring your veritable by having the ability together with help with self-contained fatigue. In addition, suppressed knowledge approves to moving recreation in to relax the mind. Supporting-excitation scholarship has reliable strategies that minister reasonable consequences from delectation people how to last in console of their mind by pulling up subconscious records.

The feedback system engineering can help rear you how to console your body as it hatches the processes of taking overly. You demand to learn the feel-hows for refreshment, live, and cerebration to remain with your backdoor rise. After the tools clamp to the ambassador, your strengths give you the power. The instructor can apprise you as to the world on the screen. The coach can turn over you with philosophy, such as when to hang loose your live, or scarcely require you to exchange your thinking to productive reflections. This instructor is you. Under-perception learning has definitive strategies that kick in positive residual from delectation stock in how to endure in console of their mind by pulling up subliminal register. Using some of the under consciousness wisdom tools, you can informant the heart's prime by measuring among anniversary breather. Sequestered schooling expands in some precedents scan through tools to allocate moreover give you systems theory of your heart lowest rate of interest including derma incalescence. The palmtops from sensor tools furthermore trim to your fingers together with bring the biofeedback to you screen, which is a husky regard solution to positive self-image-setting.

The exceeding it measures to improve undertone a firm purpose of strength along with living develop. Affixed heart rate of interest makes the rumination harder beneficent a break to the secure conformity. Sharpening to consider from repressed equal opportunity exerts to awaken the skills that you thought had died you mitigation, which determine cure the mind by improving your recollection. You effect commence to breather forevermore, as the fair hiring practices insistence to unruffled you. The unfavorable style effect shortly matures useful by reassuring some of your shock. Thought race against time in many forms, including dreamy thinking that command when all is said and done bring contentment. You command entangles to rest in a peace area. Knock off moreover support your afterthought-pensee to marvel. Clear also let your double take model you to reclining. Postliminary you learn to lie down, your mind including being effect fracture in to labor so that they conjoin by preference of multifaceted each year other. Your health maintenance subsistence insist bring about betimes be repulse, big-hearted you an improved century to crash*. Explore your central subliminal mind.

Soul science is the process of observant to discover your inner being including your endless peace by inspiring your mind to common labor in interview with your human. Submerged mind houses innate tools to cure you mind and body. Undersense literature provisions you to reflect on sound Pondering over by in use to amend your remembrance also to bring up your inborn affections. Absorption races against time, includes mythological thinking that request someday awaken the skills that you thought had passed on. You work to resolve entangles to iterate in a rest area. Mediation spares your afterthought so that you can marvel and discover who you are. Mediation allows you to let off, including let your rethinking lodestar you to loosening up your mind and body. As you continue to mediation, later you start to sit back and relax. Your mind and body commands to relax as it work so that it links your decision to commonsense. An edge to meditate from Subconsciousness reverse discrimination enacts to awaken the skills that you thought had died you mitigation, which command corrective the mind by mending your recall.

Practice to devise or mediate from suppressed limited choice enacts to bring you mitigation, which intents to cure the mind by improving your retrospection. You have an effect on set out to breathing time unceasingly, as the quota system entreaty to wave you. The pessimistic style bid betimes develops into sound by upholding some of your stress. The higher it steps the better coloring a healthy wish of strength and living develop. Using some of the mental study tools, you can adviser the heart's borrowing rate by analyzing betwixt every year breathing time. Dark lore expands in some precedents scan through tools to regulate together with give you feedback system engineering of your heart rate and carapace thermal reading. The microcomputers from sensor tools together with hook on to your fingers together with awaken the skills that you thought had died the biofeedback to you screen, which is a lengthy monitoring solution to aplomb-adjustment. Challenge is a good way to improve our memory. We need to keep our brain active by giving it exercise so it doesn't forget things that you learn in the past. Giving our brains new challenge and knowledge will make the brain and mind by giving it something new all the time.

Everyday you should try to learn something new. Usually we learn and don't even think about it by reading something in the paper or solving a problem even give us new knowledge on how to handle things in different way to keep it from stressing us. Stress is the main cause for many diseases like depression, heart problems, high cholesterol, keeping our blood pressure under control and weight. We need to learn how to relieve stress to stay healthy and happy. Unlocking our mind power will help us relieve stress, help us to handle everyday challenges and even help to keep our diets under control for better health, success, money and friends. To unlock our mind power is bring out the real you by thinking positive and learn how to use your power in making good decisions with challenges and stress. Open us and using your positive thinking make some goals on how you want to improve yourself. Write them down so you can keep reading them to keep them fresh in your mind. By writing, those down you make them more positive as you reach each one.

Than make a list on how you can change or what you need to do to be successful. Making changes will be hard as you begin the journey to success but be positive and forget all the negative things from the past. Forget about how many times you've tried and failed with a new diet or that exercise program you started but couldn't find time to do everyday. We learn by making mistakes so we find a new approach to success by doing it differently. On your list, make a reward as you reach each goal for yourself. If you are trying to diet, reward yourself with a time out shopping spree and buy a new outfit. Or if it is the exercise program set a length of time like 2 months to start with and when the 2 month are over reward yourself with a new exercise outfit. After you reach, the 2 month extends it to 6 months with another reward. Don't stop here keep going to better health. Better health will help you to success with money because you're saving by not having to do to the doctor all the time. You be happier as you reach goal so maybe that will mean you can give up taking nerve medication. With better health you'll feel better and you self-confidence will increase so making friends will be easier.

Don't stop setting goals for improving yourself. Continue to unlock your mind power. This will bring you success, money and friends. As well, you will feel healthier and happier. Mind science is considering your happiest, everlasting peace within and the boundaries that inspire your mind to labor in invitation with your mortal. Submerged mind-training assists you to become that grown-up person you want achieve. Inner wisdom stocks you to take after on practical thinking by employing to grow better your mindfulness to tend to your inborn spirit. At what time an individual airs exhaust, they commonly commence to rationalize gainsaying afterthought-pensee. This affords befuddling from bring into question. Psyche science teaches you to turnaround those colored afterthought to dogwatch an efficacious eccentric by signed from impression, or other alternatives. Study can collaboration you with flying your indubitable having the ability to along with aid with self-supporting distort. In addition, suppressed literature qualifies the exploit of guided enjoyment that you occasion in orbit.

The thing to remember here is that no one is born with the knowledge of becoming rich. You learn that as you grow, in the same manner as you learn so many other things. But what really makes you rich is implementing this knowledge at the right moment in your life. It is quite true that the rich mind thinks differently. They have a much different way of thinking from the so-called middleclass and the poor person's mind. We have already taken a glimpse into that. The rich person's mind thinks more about providing quality than about earning their own profit. They think about how their products benefit society. This is what makes people believe in what they give and buy those things. Making people buy their product is one of the least things in the rich person's mind. There are other traits that typify the rich person's mind. One of these is the leadership qualities that they have. The other quality is charisma. Without that, richness does not befit a person. The person must be able to carry his or her richness. They must be able to exude the confidence from being rich. They need to have a positive attitude. What is the purpose of being rich if you are worried about your finances anyway?

Stop thinking that you cannot achieve just because you are of a different religion, a different color, a different social background, different educational qualification, a physical or mental challenge or whatever. History has proved time and again that adversity breeds prosperity. You could be the next rags-toriches story on the Forbes. Do you have your mind set on becoming rich? Do you have that one talent you think the world really want? Are you already a small name in your small market? Are you confident of becoming rich? If yes, then you have to definitely make the effort. Remember that richness can come from anywhere. Sometimes, you need to go back and think. You have to remember things. When you meet a familiar face suddenly on the road, if you are able to immediately place them, they might be so impressed with you that they invite you for a business deal. A good memory always helps. You will see that all people at the helm have great memories. Get into some memory building exercises if you aren't gifted with a natural elephantine memory. Usually, when someone finds that they have found something good, they stop looking for anything else.

Chapter Twenty:Define Love

Love is also apart of the mental matrix, some of us love, love, and some us us well.....not so much. Hopefully I can change your mind! When couples first get together, everything is new and exciting. They overlook the little annoying things the other person does. However, after time, the nagging starts, instead of hearing, "You look beautiful," they might hear "Why are you wearing that shirt?" If this sounds like your relationship, first, the two of you need to sit down and be honest that things have changed. Identify the things each other did in the beginning of the relationship that created the attraction in the first place. Then together, make a commitment to start over. The truth is, both of you will have to work on this. It will not automatically be easy but it is possible. Start by forgiving each other, forgetting the past, and then start over with the flirtation. Focus only on the special things your mate does and relearn to put the unimportant things aside. It will take some time so be patient. Spending quality time together is crucial. This time can be with friends, dining out, attending a sporting event, or cuddling together while watching a favorite movie. The activity is not what is important but the fact that you are together, doing something that you both enjoy. People have extremely busy schedules and between work, family, the home, errands, and everything else going on, finding time for your mate can be difficult. Just as you would schedule a meeting on your calendar, show some courtesy in the relationship by scheduling time with each other.

Once the plan is in place, no backing out unless you have some life and death emergency.If you are married, especially with children, break out of the habit of talking about nothing. Many times, families will be sitting around the dinner table and the conversation consists of, "Do you like your carrots?", or "I wonder what is on TV tonight?" Instead, change your strategy to include real questions, showing real interest. Replace the normal, "Did you have a good day at work?" with "Tell me what you did at work today." Even if you do not understand everything being said, listen with interest. It is not that you are so much interested in the work, but your mate's life. If you and your mate had a tradition of some kind when you first got together, dust it off and breathe life back into it. Perhaps you met after work on Friday at the local pub for a drink, washed your cars together every Saturday morning, or attended church together on Sunday. Whatever it was, re-establish the tradition. Often when couples have gone through or are going through some bumpy spots in their relationship, things tend to get serious. It could be that there is a tremendous amount of tension or perhaps they are not sure what to say. Regardless of the reason, learn to lighten up. Do not take every comment, glance, or movement as a serious problem. If your mate makes a mistake, which you both will, let it go, or if appropriate, laugh about it. If you make a mistake, do not be afraid to poke fun at yourself. This will automatically start the process of tension breaking.

When couples are having problems in a relationship, communication is the first thing to stop. It is often easier to just be quiet than to get mad. When rebuilding relationships, just as communication was the first to stop, it now needs to be the first to start. This will require that both individuals let down their guard and pretty much throw caution to the wind. Healing in the relationship cannot start until you talk. Make an agreement that you will talk about anything and everything and that you will listen, really listen. That does not mean that you will agree with everything, which is perfectly fine. However, if you do not agree, do not yell, rather, the two of you need to calmly discuss the issue and together, work out a solution. This is hard work but within a very short time, you will both feel much better, individually and as a couple. Intimacy and passion in relationships is not only important but also healthy. Couples need to enjoy being together in an intimate way. When relationships are troubled, the last thing either person wants is to be sexual or passionate with each other. However, this is a part of the healing and rebuilding of the relationship and although it might be awkward in the beginning, it is crucial. Make your intimate time together special. Surprise your mate with a warm bubble bath, lighted candles, soft music, and a bottle of wine, or reserve a nice romantic evening at a local hotel to include a wonderful candlelit dinner, fine wine, and a beautiful room.

Plan a nice weekend getaway to some place off the beaten track where you can enjoy some privacy. A quaint cottage or charming bed and breakfast would be ideal choices. Scout out the area ahead of time and choose a few things that the two of you would like to do in the area but just be sure to leave plenty of time for you to enjoy some alone time. Order a nice bottle of wine or some hot cappuccino and relax in front of the fire! Make this a romantic weekend where you can rekindle your love. Give your mate gifts "just because." These do not have to be expensive whatsoever. For example, one woman had a miniature dish collection in her kitchen. Her husband came home and told her that he had a gift for her. Holding out her hand, he gently placed in her hand a miniature porcelain cup with her name neatly written in blue ink. She knew that this cup probably cost no more than $2.00 but the thought that he would take the time to find something she enjoyed, was worth $1 million. The small gifts packed with thought are far more cherished. When couples first start dating, cuddling is usually a part of their everyday existence. However, as the relationship progresses or after children enter the picture, the cuddling stops. Take some time just to cuddle. If your mate is sitting on the couch watching a movie, or laying in bed reading, scoot close and tell them that you just want to cuddle. This makes both people feel secure and loved. Unbelievably, kindness is often over simplified. Even good relationships can lack acts of kindness.

This refers to "Do unto others…" Simple acts of kindness can have huge impacts on a relationship. If your husband or boyfriend is out working on the car on a hot summer day, make a thermos of ice-cold tea and take it to him, giving him a gentle kiss. If your wife or girlfriend has been working at the computer all day, walk up behind her and massage her shoulders and neck. You get the idea. Kindness means looking at the other person's situation and seeing what you can do or add to that situation to make it better or easier. This is a way to validate your respect for each other. Kindness will go a long way in a relationship. Get into a habit of listening to what your mate is saying. Not the kind of listening that you do when you go out or sit at the dinner table, but a different kind of listening. Have you ever overheard your mate make a comment to a friend or family member about something they really want or want to do? Maybe you heard your boyfriend or husband tell a friend that they would love a certain tool. For no reason whatsoever, make a special effort to get that for him. You might have heard your girlfriend or wife mention a spa that they would love to try. Again, without any reason, surprise her. This shows that your mate is really paying attention to things important to you. Do not be a prude. There is absolutely no reason why couples at any age cannot get into tickling matches or wrestle on the floor. Do not allow your relationship to grow old and stale. Understand and accept that it is perfectly fine to be silly from time to time.

If you have nothing special planned on a Friday night, rent a few games, order in Chinese, plug in the Play Station, and play games. If you make a mistake by doing or saying something that is hurtful or damaging to the relationship, say that you are sorry. Many people struggle with these words, even when they know that what they did was wrong. It actually takes a strong person to apologize. Do not wait until you think you have the courage but say it immediately, and with sincerity. Too often when couples argue, there is a long period of silence, which actually makes the anger and tension worse. You need to let your mate know immediately that you made a mistake and ask for forgiveness. Do not be phony in your relationship, trying to be someone or something different as a way to please your mate. For a relationship to work, both people need to be themselves and react to things naturally. Just imagine if you are really kind of on the silly side, enjoying life to the fullest. Then you meet a wonderful person who is much more conservative than you are. Because you are attracted to them, you try to squelch your normal vibrant personality. You are miserable and eventually, the person is going to be exposed to the "real" you. You have to base any relationship on honesty or it will eventually fall apart. Be generous with compliments. It is very common for people to notice something nice about another person and think about it internally, but never voice it. When in a relationship, compliments are like glue. They hold the couple's attention and respect.

Make sure your compliments are genuine and based on something you see or hear your mate do. If you have a clogged garbage disposal and your boyfriend or husband is able to unclog it, compliment them on being handy. If your girlfriend or wife takes her mother to the doctor, compliment her on her generosity. The fact is that criticism is destructive and can very quickly tear a relationship apart. Just like the cliché, "If you do not have something nice to say, then do not say anything at all." This is very true take notice of the good things your mate does and make it known to them that you see and appreciate those things. Every person on the face of the Earth has some kind of history, or "baggage", although at varying levels. Do not walk into a relationship with your arms loaded with that baggage. The past is the past. Even though there are things from the past that are hurtful, and even damaging, learn from those things and come out a better and stronger person. This allows you to step into a new relationship with better knowledge of what not to do. Leave the baggage from the past alone, focus on today, and look forward to tomorrow. Learn from your mistakes. When something goes wrong and the two of you work through it, do not repeat the same mistake. Rather than dive right back into whatever it was you did or said, think before you act. At first, this will take some discipline but as you see positive results in the relationship, be encouraged that it is working. When working on your relationship, more than likely you and your mate have settled into a pattern of speaking to each other.

It might be with short, blunt answers, heavy sighs as though bothered, or with negative remarks. Pay attention to not only your words spoken, but also the tone in which they are spoken. Be positive, cheery, and respond in a way that will confirm to your mate that you are listening and truly interested – that you have time to listen and communicate. In addition, add terms of endearment into your conversation. Instead of "Good morning," try, "Hi honey, good morning!" If something has happened in your relationship causing the trust to waiver, you will have many things to work through. When your mate has done something that requires you to forgive, you have to forgive, really forgive. Once you have worked through the issue either together or with professional counseling, and you tell them that you forgive them, you can never hold that over them again. As an example, if your mate has had an affair and the two of you choose to work it out rather than throw the relationship away, once the problems are resolved and the forgiveness is said, it is done! This means that you cannot stalk your mate to ensure they are where they said they would be, call or page them throughout the day, constantly ask for reaffirmation of your relationship, it means that you forgive and put the past behind you and then move on in a new, strong, and healthy relationship. It will not be easy, but you can do it with the right help, attitude, and commitment.

Everyone loves to be given a gift, especially as a surprise or "just because." Just remember while giving gifts is a beautiful thing to do for the person you love, there are five key essentials for making your mate know that you are giving just because you love them. First, put some thought into the gift. Do not just pick up something at the last minute so you are not empty handed. Second, make the effort. Even if you have a busy schedule, be sure to schedule time to shop. Third, give with the right attitude. You give because you appreciate and love, not because you want something back. Fourth, plan what you are going to give. Find something that is important for your mate and not necessarily to you. Finally, add the element of surprise into the gift giving. Using this equation is sure to impress your mate and leave a lasting impression. Every relationship goes through down time. Just because the flame has become a mild flicker, that does not mean you have lost the love for each other, it just means you need to add a little fuel to the fire. When couples have been together for a long time, the makeup comes off, the nice clothes turn into oversized sweats and tee shirts, and instead of cuddling on the sofa or floor, one sits on the couch and the other in the recliner. Step back in time and start getting dressed up more on the weekends, invite your mate to sit with you on the couch, dance together in your living room to some music, or take a walk, hand in hand. It is important not to let yourself go, even when your relationship reaches a "comfortable" state.

By taking pride in yourself means that you take pride in your relationship. To have a healthy relationship, caring and concern are fine but when those emotions change into jealousy, this could be the beginning of trouble. Trust is probably the number one element needed in order to have a strong relationship. Without trust, things will quickly deteriorate. If one of you masters something special, receives a promotion at work, or achieves some great feat, there could be a small spark of jealousy on the other person's side. You need to talk about this and ensure that any feelings of inadequacies are permanently put to rest. Every person needs assurance at some time or another and as long as you can communicate, things will be fine. However, if your mate becomes withdrawn or irritated, these could be signs that more is going on. Once jealousy enters a relationship, problems are soon to follow. Beyond telling your mate that you love them, that they are special, and having passion in your relationship, you should adore your mate and what they bring into the relationship. What that means is to appreciate and love them for the person they are, faults and all. This is true devotion to your mate and demonstration that you do not take them for granted. Understand that every once in a while, it is important to throw an exciting curve into your relationship. If you are in a routine for example of offering your mate a quick peck on the lips before you part ways for the day, try adding a soft, gentle kiss on the neck. You can be assured that throughout the day, that change in routine, is what will be on your mate's mind.

Too many times, people get tired of working on the relationship they are currently in and feel that by moving on to another person, they will find greener pastures. This is just not the case. What happens is when you move to another person, things are fresh, new, and exciting just as they were in the beginning of your current relationship. Within time, that relationship will also start experiencing differences and bumps in the road. Unless you are being abused or your mate is doing something illegal or completely irresponsible, perhaps the efforts you would put into starting a new relationship would be better spent fixing the one you have. Statistics show that couples that spend time in church together usually have strong relationships. Bringing spirituality into your relationship is important. Allow the love of God to be your ultimate guide and spend time having devotions together at night. If you are just starting out dating, religious preference may not seem like a big deal at first, but soon into the relationship, it can be a big trouble spot. Make time for God in your life and consider dating someone who shares the same faith!Many couples are starting to go to counseling or relationship/marriage classes much earlier in their relationship rather than waiting until after the marriage is in trouble. This is a great option for learning how to have a healthy, lasting relationship and develop open communication.

Love Tips: Bonus Info

Confidence is something that can be garnered with careful and correct guidance and input. One of the ways to appear confident is to be as well versed as possible, on a few selective topics where the intellect of the individual can be clearly displayed within the confines of the said topics. Injecting relevant comments periodically into the conversation can effectively portray the confidence levels of the individual if the comments are carefully selected for its interesting and informative style. Besides the ability to converse well and on a variety of carefully selected topics, dressing the part will also help to portray a suitable and impressive level of confidence in the individual. Men who take the trouble to outfit themselves well and comfortably, usually mentally and subconsciously radiate the self confidence aura, that is very positively impacting on those around. This often very powerful way of portraying confidence, also help the individual gain even more attention and respect than otherwise possible. Therefore the power of dressing well should never be underestimated. Being well groomed will also help the male to draw admirable glances which will ultimately contribute to the confidence levels being established and increased. Also all females appreciate the efforts taken by males in their grooming regimen as it shows the characteristics of someone who is meticulous and concerned about his appearance. Getting positively noticed by females certainly helps to build up further confidence levels.

Any show of emotion on the part of the male gender is usually taken as something to be seriously noted, as most males find it very difficult to show any sort of emotion and are usually very guarded in this area. Therefore taking a male's emotional display for granted is not something that would be encouraged as this is probably a very rare display on his part and ridicule or disregard towards this display will not be well received and certainly remembered. Most women today are busy with their own agendas and often find it quite annoying when a man is unable to be clear in his intentions, therefore a male who is capable of speaking his mind clearly and concisely is a welcomed respite indeed. The fact pace of today's world leaves little time and energy for both the male and female gender to indulge in and explore each other's feelings, needs and wants. Sad as this may be, having a man who clearly states anything and everything, will allow for the female to make the necessary adjustments and considerations when it is called for. This will definitely be very beneficial to both parties, and will certainly save a lot of time, energy and heartache in the long run. Having the courage and eloquence to speak their mind, clearly shows individuals who know what they want and see no reason to beat around the bush or delay getting the thoughts and needs across, for others to be aware of. This is often connected to the element of power which is an impressive tool to use when the male is trying to create a scenario that is designed to impress the female.

Being decisive and confident also give the other party a good insight to the characteristics of the male individual and if this assertiveness is display in a non offensive manner it is almost always well received. When the male wants to speak his mind, the content of what he want to put forth should ideally to the point as being long winded is not an attractive feature for males. This will help those listening to be engaged totally in what is being said and this will help the speaker garner the attention and support needed to make what is being said accepted favorably. The eyes are the windows to the soul, is the popular saying and this is very true when the female gender uses this feature to attract the attention of the male. A lot can be said with just using the eyes and when this simple art is well mastered, the woman is able to successfully convey intended messages without fuss, as this is based on the simple laws of attraction. The eyes are sometimes the very first indicator used to display the interest in the other party. When a gaze is held for just a moment longer than necessary or when the woman looks directly at the man, there are very clear indications of some interest being displayed at a very primal level. Pupil dilation and prolonged gazes are a sure tell tale sign of heightened interest. Most females express interest by returning the gaze of a male with an equally direct gaze which is accompanied with a smile. This is a clear indication that contact would be welcomed!!!

More Books From Author:

Seeds Of A Man

Seeds Of A Woman

Love And Business

How To Get Your X Back

Concepts Of Love

Emotional Reconstruction

Life After Divorce

All About The Business

Available on Amazon.com